E-Z Review™

for

Administrative Law

Original Manuscript By

Randy J. Riley, Esq.
Seton Hall University Law School

Contributing Editor:

Adam C. Rhea, Esq.
University of Virginia Law School

Consulting Editor
Stephen H. Ruderman, Esq.

Law Review Publishing
New York, NY 10010
800-371-1271

www.lawreviewpublishing.com

Visit our website for updates
www.lawreviewpublishing.com

TABLE OF CONTENTS

I. HISTORICAL OVERVIEW

This section provides a historical overview of administrative law and its statutory basis. In addition, the section briefly discusses the rise of the popularity of agencies and examines how traditional and modern views of agencies have evolved.

A. History of Administrative Law

Administrative law is a comparatively recent development in the law, and is one that continues to evolve.

1. Traditional View

a. 1800's

There were very few administrative agencies in the 1800's. Those that did exist had very little power.

b. Early 1900's

In the early 1900's the concept of administrative law blossomed, largely as the result of President Franklin D. Roosevelt's progressive legislation known popularly as the "New Deal." The New Deal vastly expanded social legislation, and many different agencies came into being as a result. Along with the agency came administrative powers which were lacking in the 1800's.

2. Modern Interpretation

a.   The field of administrative law greatly expanded in the 1960's and 1970's as a result of the social agenda of the Kennedy and Johnson administrations. President Johnson, especially, involved the government in many different social areas which resulted in the extension of administrative law.

b.   In the 1980's a reversal in the trend of administrative expansion began. This era was marked by the derogatory term "Big Government," and was characterized by controls being set up to limit the power of agencies. Under the new legislation, before agencies could implement regulations they were required to perform a cost-benefit analysis. Legislators decided in many areas to deregulate, resulting in the agencies losing considerable power and influence.

c.   The 1990's saw a dramatic change in social legislation (e.g. welfare, immigration), without a corresponding change in the character of the administrative agencies, and without a reduction in the need for administrative agencies.

Note.   Every change in the character of the government brings with it a decided change in the view of the meaning of administrative regulation.

---

4.   Administrative Procedure Act (APA)
The APA was written after World War II in an effort to protect due process for people affected by the decisions of agencies. The APA's main function is a guideline of procedural rules for administrative agencies.

See Appendix for the text of The APA.

5.   Administrative Procedure Act of 1946 (APA), Purpose
The Administrative Procedure Act outlines administrative procedures that federal agencies should follow such as:

§§ 551-559, 701-706, 1305, 3344, 4301, 5362, 7521, and 60 Stat. 237 as amended by PL 79-404	Identify information to be made public Publish material in the *Federal Register* Maintain records, including those involving certain meetings and hearings Notice requirements Issue licenses Review agency actions

The Act also grants the public certain rights to participate in rulemaking and to speak during adjudications.

B. Agency Regulations

The agency may perform its mission in several ways. Most often, the agency the authority delegated to it by Congress by either 1) granting licenses, 2) making a rule to give effect to legislation, or 3) by deciding the merits of individual cases (adjudicating) on an ad hoc basis.

1. Rulemaking.

Rulemaking is facially similar to law-making. The agency decides on a new rule it wants to implement, then (as we shall see) gives notice to the public and provides an opportunity for comment. The agency then decides on a course of action and publishes the rule (generally in the Federal Register).

2. Adjudications.

When an agency feels a particular regulation has been violated, or in the absence of a rule covering the situation, the agency has the power to hold a quasi-judicial proceeding called an adjudication. The agency has the power to decide the case and impose civil penalties. Administrative decisions are given great deference in most instances.

II. DELEGATION AND SEPARATION OF POWERS

This section deals with the creation and powers of the agency, the formation and employment of agencies, the types of power that may be delegated, limitations upon the on the delegation of power, and powers retained by Congress.

A. Delegation

1. Overview

Panama Refining v. Ryan, 293 U.S. 388 (1935)
Facts: Texas passed laws purporting to control the production of oil within its borders. Congress then passed a law which allowed the President virtually unlimited discretion to stop production of oil in any state which had prohibited interstate sale of the oil.
Held: The Supreme Court decided that the Congressional delegation of unfettered power to the President was in conflict with the Constitutional system of "Separation of Powers." The Court noted that any delegation of discretionary power must be accompanied by limits or guidelines on that power.

Schecter Poultry Corp. v. U.S., 295 U.S. 495, 55 S. Ct. 837 (1935)
Facts: Congress passed a law which authorized the President to promulgate regulations on fair competition. The President, pursuant to this power, passed several regulations concerning fair competition, resulting in the Schecter Poultry Corporation's prosecution for a violation.
Held: The Supreme Court held that the statute granting the authority to the President was unconstitutional. The Court held that the law was in essence a grant of absolute power without any checks or balances. The Court noted that the grant of power was unrestrained in that Congress gave no standards or guidelines in its implementation. Furthermore, the delegation of power was not accompanied by any administrative procedures on the adoption or implementation of the regulations.

2. Delegation of Authority

Industrial Union Department, AFL-CIO v. API, 448 U.S. 607 (1980)

Facts: OSHA passed several regulations relating to the health and safety of workers. One such regulation allowed the Secretary of Labor to set the standard for carcinogens in the workplace. OSHA determined that Benzene, at high levels, causes cancer and allowed the Secretary of Labor to set strict standards to prevent exposure. As a result, most companies utilizing Benzene could not meet the standard and could not afford to make the changes to comply.

Held: The Supreme Court struck down the regulation of the Secretary of Labor. The Court held that a cost-benefit analysis had to be performed. The Court held that the granting statute meant that OSHA (or its delegate) need not make the workplace Benzene-free but rather as safe as economically feasible. The Court held that OSHA, due to the wording in the grant of authority from Congress, could not set a standard that was not economically feasible.

a. **Test**
   i. Is the regulation necessary? If the answer is yes, then go to (ii) below. If the answer is no, then the regulation is invalid.
   ii. Is there a significant risk of harm? If the answer is yes, then go to (iii) below. If the answer is no, then the regulation is invalid.
   iii. Does the risk of harm outweigh the costs of compliance? If the answer is yes, the regulation is valid. If the answer is no, then the regulation is invalid.

B. Separation of Powers- Legislative Branch

1. Oversight of Agencies

A key issue in separation of powers cases concerns oversight of agencies to ensure that they act in a proper manner. Most agencies are under the Executive Branch, although some are independent. Congress naturally wants to maintain a degree of control over those to whom it delegates the authority to see compliance with the laws it passes. As a result, there is controversy as to who should have the control and who actually controls.

a. Congress delegates authority to interpret and enforce legislation.

b. Congress retains budget authority in setting the agency's operating budget. If Congress does not like the actions of the agency it can cut the agency's budget to restrain its power.

c. Congress also sometimes dictates the agency's life span via a "sunset law," which occurs when Congress grants power to a new agency, but limits the existence of the agency to a fixed term of years. When the time comes for termination, Congress must pass a new law re-authorizing the agency's existence for another term of years. As a result, if the agency oversteps it bounds, then time will terminate its existence in the absence of a re-authorization law.

d. However, Congress cannot side-step the law by creating a "legislative veto.". A legislative veto occurs pursuant to legislation allowing one house of Congress to vote to overturn an agency decision.

e. Creation

Congress creates agencies by passing enacting legislation and presenting it to the President, who signs it into law, or by overriding a Presidential veto. The agency has several distinct roles. One part is enforcement and investigation, one part is legislative, and the other part is judicial.

Immigration and Naturalization Service (INS) v. Chadha, 462 U.S. 919 (1983)
Facts: Congress delegated its authority to the INS regarding the promulgation of immigration regulations and their enforcement and adjudication. However, if Congress disagreed with an action of the INS then by statute one or both Houses could vote to override the action (a legislative veto provision). An INS administrative judge ruled Chadha had met the requirements for hardship and suspended deportation. The House of Representatives used its legislative veto power and ordered the deportation.

Held: The Supreme Court held the legislative veto unconstitutional. The Court noted that the power violated the Presentment Clause as well as the Constitutional requirement of bicameralism because Congress retained the power to essentially make unicameral law without the President being a part of the process. Congress has the power to set the standards when it delegates to another branch, but once that power has been delegated Congress cannot retain that power. Congress' only option is to change the law by passing legislation and presenting it to the President again.

Bowsher v. Synar, 478 U.S. 714 (1986)
Facts: Congress passed several statutes to control the rapidly rising federal deficit. One of the statutes called for the Office of Management and Budget to determine the deficit. OMB would then report to the Comptroller General who would review, cut the budget, cut program funding and finally send the determination to the President who was to carry out the report's findings. The statute allowed for the Comptroller General to be appointed by the President but removable only by Congress.
Held: The Supreme Court held the removal power of Congress violated the Separation of Powers doctrine. The Court held that an Executive Branch official cannot be removed by Congress except through the impeachment process. The Court noted that to allow this type of removal power would significantly interfere with the Executive Branch's ability to carry out its constitutional powers.

Note. SIGNIFICANCE
The Court used a formal test to find if the Constitution delegates that authority.

Plaut v. Spendthrift Farm, 115 S. Ct. 1447 (1995)
Facts: In certain enabling legislation, Congress set a limitations period for the agency's judicial action. The statute of limitations had run so that Spendthrift Farms could not be sued. Congress subsequently passed another law that expanded the statute of limitations and allowed the suit.
Held: The Supreme Court struck down the suit, holding that while Congress can expand the statute of limitations, it cannot make such an expansion retroactive.

2. Strauss Theory

Congress has created these agencies through law. These agencies have the power to legislate, enforce and interpret the law and the subsequent regulations. Because the original law was properly passed, the mixing of the agency's functions is also proper. The only restraint on the agency's actions is the requirement that its actions conform to the intent and purpose of the original enacting statute by Congress.

3. Court Review of Action

a. If a court invalidates an agency action it usually does so under the separation of powers doctrine if a court upholds an agency action then the court usually applies a more functional test, and generally approves the action as pursuant to the "necessary and proper" clause of the Constitution by deferring to the agency's interpretation.

C. Separation of Powers - Executive Branch

Myers v. U.S., 272 U.S. 52, 47 S. Ct. 21 (1926)

Facts: A law creating the position of Postmaster General directed the Postmaster General would be a high ranking official in the Executive Branch. In the legislation, Congress stated the Postmaster General could only be removed from office with two-thirds consent of the Senate.

Held: The Supreme Court held the removal power to be unconstitutional. The Court held that the Constitution grants the President the power to appoint and remove high-ranking executive members, and this law was in conflict with the President's Article II powers.

Humphrey's Executor v. United States, 295 U.S. 602 (1935)

Facts: A statute enabling the Federal Trade Commission called for the commission to be headed by the Federal Trade Commissioner. The Commissioner was to be a high-ranking, Executive branch member. The statute expressly limited his removal by the President to "for good cause" reasons. Due to a difference in political thinking, President Roosevelt fired the FTC Commissioner without "good cause".

Held: The Supreme Court struck down the "for good cause" requirement. The Court held that it impermissibly interfered with the President's constitutional right to appoint/remove high-ranking Executive officials and violated the Separation of Powers doctrine.

Morrison v. Olson, 487 U.S 654 (1988)

Facts: Congress passed an Ethics in Government Act that directed the Attorney General, at the request of Congress, to appoint an independent counsel to oversee different executive offices (in this case the EPA). The independent counsel reported to Congress.

Held: The Supreme Court held this to be constitutional. The Court noted that the Constitution gave the President the power to appoint/remove only high ranking executive officers and not inferior officers. The Court held the action did not impermissibly infringe upon the President's Article II powers.

Note. SIGNIFICANCE

The Court utilized a functional test. This is a test examining powers not expressly addressed in the Constitution. The question is whether is whether legislation is necessary for the effectuation of the agency's mission, and whether exercise of that delegated power impermissibly burdens the power of another branch.

III. AGENCIES' POWERS

The agency deals with a variety of issues in many ways; to include formal or informal rulemaking, as well as formal or informal adjudication. Each demands due process, but the exact level differs. This section explores those differences.

A. Due Process - Procedural Issues

Londoner v. Denver, 210 U.S. 373 (1908)

Facts: A Colorado state statute empowered the Denver board of public works to make local improvements and assess the cost against property that was benefited. The process did not allow residents an opportunity to be heard before decisions were made.

Held: The Supreme Court held the process to be unconstitutional as a denial of due process. The Court noted that the action may take place, but the city council as a representative of the state must provide for a hearing after proper notice. At the hearing, the residents must be given an opportunity to be heard.

Bi-Metallic Investment Company v. State Board of Equalization of Colorado, 239 U.S. 441 (1915)

Facts: The state of Colorado sought to increase the valuation of all taxable property in Denver by 40%. An owner of property that would be affected sued to enjoin the increase, claiming he was not given an opportunity to be heard.

Held: The Supreme Court ruled that where the agency's action would affect the whole populace, an individualized hearing was not necessary. The Court noted that all the property owners are affected and a hearing for each would be counter-productive. The Court assumed for purposes of this case that the normal administrative procedures for a collective hearing were followed, and expressly narrowed the issue to whether each individual concerned has a constitutional right to be heard before a matter can be decided when all are equally affected.

1. **Criteria for Procedures**

   What are the criteria for evaluating procedural systems by the courts?

   a. *Accuracy*: measures whether the action taken is rational to meet the goals.

   b. *Efficiency*: measures whether the action taken will overburden the system if individualized hearings are required.

   c. *Acceptability*: measures whether the procedures that are followed are sufficient to be considered fair to the community.

2. **Londoner/Bi-Metallic Rule**

   There is a difference between rulemaking and adjudication as discussed by the respective cases. If an agency's action is directed to an individual ex post, the action is generally deemed adjudicative in nature. If the agency's action concerns the prospective general treatment of persons, the agency's action will likely be considered rule-making

3. **APA § 551**

   a. *Rule*
   Rulemaking is utilized where the effect of agency action on persons will occur in the future. In this type of case, rulemaking is necessary to achieve the goal.

   b. *Order*
   An order denotes a disposition of a particular case and is associated with an adjudicative function.

Formal and Informal Rulemaking – Applicable APA Sections

	Rulemaking	Adjudication
Informal	**ALL:** § 552(a)(1) - publication § 553(e) – petition to alter or repeal the rules. **SUBSTANTIVE:** Notice, Opportunity, Publication of purpose, § 553(d) – At least a 30 day delay between publication and effective dates.	N/A
Formal	§553(b) – Notice § 556 – Opportunity to comment § 557 – Intermediate and Final Decision on wording of Rule § 553(d)- At least a 30 day delay between publication and effectiveness §552(a)(1) - Publication. §553(e) – Petition to issue, amend or repeal a Rule	§554 – Notice, settlement negotiations, hearing. §556 – Hearing. §557 – Adjudication §554(e) – Order.

American Medical Association v. United States, 887 F.2d 760 (7th Cir. 1989).

Facts: The AMA was a tax-exempt organization in the United States, which published medical periodicals paid for by advertising. The IRS ruled the advertising was not related to the AMA's tax-exempt educational mission and was therefore taxable. The IRS proposed rules to govern the allocation of revenues and expenses in this type of situation. The AMA did not comment on the proposed rule but other organizations which were similarly situated did. The IRS formulated a rule allowing three permissible arrangements. The proposed rule and the final rule were different, but related. The AMA challenged the final rule based on lack of notice.

Held: The court held that the issue of notice requires only that the parties affected by the final rule be put on notice that their "interest" was at stake. The court held that the AMA was on notice that taxing advertising income was the issue. The court concluded that the AMA had notice of any rule which was the "logical outgrowth" of the original proposal.

National Black Media v. FCC, 791 F.2d 1016 (2nd Cir. 1986).

Facts: The FCC had a policy that allowed for minority preferences in the granting of licenses. Normal policy was that any new station wishing to be licensed had to demonstrate the geographic area was undeserved or not served. The FCC policy accepted minority-owned stations. As a result of an international agreement, the FCC departed from previous policy and eliminated the minority exception.

Held: The court held the FCC failed to provide adequate notice of its decision to change policy toward minority-owned stations. The court further noted that the agency failed to consider all relevant factors in its rulemaking process. The court noted that the final rule need not duplicate the proposal, however, if the final rule significantly deviates from the original there must be another round of notice and opportunity to be heard before the rule may take effect.

    b.   *Comment* § 553(c)

        Interested parties must be given an opportunity to comment on the pending proposed rule. However, not every person who wants to comment can comment. The agency may limit the number of persons who are testifying to the same fact. Comment may mean only written comment.

See Vermont Yankee and Pension, infra, page 20.

c. **Response § 553(c)**
   After notice and comment, the agency will formulate a statement explaining the basis for the rule and its purpose.

FCC v. NCCB, 436 U.S. 775 (1978)
Facts: The FCC adopted regulations after proper notice and comment that prohibited transfer of radio or TV licenses to newspaper owners in the same community. The agency ruled that any newspaper-broadcast marriage in the past five years would also be terminated, but that such mixes more than five years old would be grandfathered. The Court of Appeals held that divestiture in this manner was arbitrary and capricious and ordered the FCC to reverse all of the divestitures.
Held: The Supreme Court agreed the proper standard was the "arbitrary and capricious" test, but did not agree with the way in which the Court of Appeals applied the test. The Court held that the FCC's reasons were rational in that new markets would not be well-served by the monopoly of newspapers and broadcast media, and that to divest the older (grandfathered) media marriages would significantly damage the community.

United States v. Nova Scotia Food Products, 568 F.2d 240 (2nd Cir. 1977).
Facts: An FDA regulation mandated that hot-processed smoked fish be heated at certain temperatures for certain lengths of time. An FDA inspection at the plant revealed that the plant was in violation of this regulation. A producer argued that the regulation precluded the production of marketable whitefish and could not be met. The producer also argued that the regulation was outside the delegated authority of the enabling statute, that the FDA relied on undisclosed evidence in promulgating the regulation, and that there was no adequate statement setting forth the basis and purpose of the regulation.
Held: The Court held that the regulation was unconstitutional because the FDA utilized undisclosed evidence in their assessment, preventing the producer from having an opportunity for meaningful comment on the proposed regulation. Also, the agency did not respond in writing as to whether the whitefish were not marketable at the temperatures regulated. The court also noted that even though this was an informal action, a record must be kept for judicial review.

Independent U.S. Tanker Owners Committee v. Dole, 809 F.2d 847
(9th Cir.), *cert. denied* , 484 U.S. 819 (1987)
Facts: In 1936, Congress passed legislation that allowed for
subsidies for construction of US ships that would operate in foreign
commerce. This was done in response to the great difficulty of
manufacturers in competing in that market, due to higher U.S. labor
costs. Even after the subsidy, the ships continued to fair worse than
their foreign counterparts Also, the US foreign ships were not
allowed to compete domestically when they received a subsidy.
However, merchant ships operating domestically did not enjoy these
subsidies. They were protected by the Jones Act which required any
cargo transported in the US to be carried by a US-built ship. In 1977,
after the opening of the Alaskan pipeline, the domestic ships had
difficulty in transporting oil to other points in the country. The
Maritime administration decided that US foreign ships could, for 6
months per year, compete domestically if they repaid the
proportional subsidy.
Held: The Supreme Court held that the rule's statement of basis and
purpose was inadequate to show why the action served the stated
goal. Furthermore, there was no statement as to why the alternative
measures were rejected in favor of the rule. Without such discussion,
the Court held that the action by the Secretary was arbitrary and
capricious.

Vermont Yankee Nuclear Power Corporation v. NRDC, 435 U.S.
519 (1978)
Facts: A nuclear power plant sought a license. The NRDC opposed
the license, and a hearing was granted. Another environmental group
sought to voice their objection to the license as well, but was
excluded from the hearing. The license was granted by the Board.
Subsequently, an oversight commission superior to the Board held an
open forum to discuss the issue. The Commission allowed many
environmental groups to speak and be heard. The power plant
operators appealed the decision, citing the propriety of the
subsequent proceeding.
Held: The Supreme Court held that additional proceedings beyond
what was set out in the enabling statute were not required.

    d.   Effects of *Vermont Yankee*:
- i.   Notice and comment were adequate for due process purposes.
- ii.   The courts and agencies could not require any further procedures for decision other than what was permitted by the enabling statute.
- iii.   The court noted that if there is any comment opposing the action then the agency must respond to those comments in writing.
- iv.   The reliance is on the statute and the APA, not judicial discretion.

Pension Benefit Guaranty Corporation v. LTC Corporation, 496 U.S. 633 (1990)
Held: The Supreme Court reaffirmed the decision in *Vermont Yankee*, holding the court system cannot impose specific procedural requirements upon an agency when there is no basis in the APA. The court's duty is to ensure that an agency action conforms to the minimum requirement of due process and that any action is not arbitrary or capricious.

   3.   **Informal Rulemaking**
      This type of rulemaking usually involves policy or interpretation. It is also known as "§ 553 Rulemaking."

C. Formal Adjudications

   1.   **Formal**
      This is a trial-type hearing and requires notice and an opportunity for a hearing with cross-examination.
      APA §§ 553, 556, and 557 are utilized.

FTC v. Cement Institute, 333 U.S. 683 (1948)
Facts: Citing evidence showing the price of cement was uniform throughout the U.S., the FTC alleged that the appellant (collection of 74 cement manufacturers) had hindered and restrained competition in violation of the FTCA. The appellant argued that its actions were not unfair, and that the FTC did not have jurisdiction and was biased.
Held: The Supreme Court held that the FTC did have jurisdiction. The Court noted the legislative history strongly suggested that the Sherman Act be enforced through other administrative agencies such as the FTC. The Court further held that the FTC was not biased and the FTC did investigate and articulate their views.

Castillio-Villagra v. INS, 972 F.2d 1017 (9th Cir. 1992)
Facts: A family unsuccessfully sought asylum, claiming a fear of persecution by the Sandinistas because of their anti-Sandinista political views. While their case was pending the Sandinista government lost the election in Nicaragua to a democratic political party. The Board of Appeals took notice of the election and concluded that because the Sandinistas lost there was no further threat. The family was not given notice or opportunity for hearing to consider whether the change of government obviated their request for asylum based upon a fear of persecution.
Held: The court reversed the Board. Noting the family was not given notice or opportunity to be heard regarding the effect of the new election, the court distinguished a legislative fact from an adjudicative fact. A legislative fact is a decision of law and policy by an agency which does not concern an individual party. An adjudicative fact is one in which the legislative fact is applied to an individual party. A legislative fact requires no notice and opportunity to be heard unless it is applied to a particular party (adjudicative). The court held that the fear of persecution was an adjudicative fact that required notice and an opportunity to be heard. The court reversed and remanded.

Director v. Greenwich Collieries, 114 S. Ct. 2251 (1994)
Facts: When adjudicating benefits under the Black Lung Benefits Act, the Dept. of Labor utilized the "true doubt rule," which shifted the burden of persuasion to the party opposing the benefits claim. Under the Labor Department's rule, if the evidence on both sides was balanced, the benefit claimant would win – a result contrary to APA § 7(c) which says that unless otherwise provided by statute the moving party has the burden of proof.
Held: The Supreme Court held the "true doubt rule" violated the APA. The Court analyzed burden of proof vs. burden of persuasion. The Court held the APA burden of proof includes burden of persuasion.

Armstrong v. CFTC, 12 F.3d 401 (3rd Cir. 1993)

Facts: CFTC charged Armstrong with failing to disclose clients and failure to register. Armstrong used three now-defunct corporations to accomplish commodities transactions. The CFTC sought to prove the individual liability of Armstrong, and the ALJ found Armstrong personally liable. On appeal the Commission found that the ALJ's opinion was substantially correct. Armstrong appealed on the basis of APA § 557(c), arguing that the Commission failed to supply an adequate "statement of ... findings and conclusions, and the reasons or basis therefore, on all the material issues of fact, law, or discretion presented on the record."

Held: The court held that the Commission need not address each individual statement if it adopts an ALJ opinion which sets forth adequate conclusions and findings. However, the Commission in this instance did not adopt the ALJ opinion in whole, and the court found "substantially correct" an insufficient standard for appellate review. The Commission must announce reasons for any dissent regarding the ALJ opinion.

Note. Formal rulemaking is needed.

United States v. Florida East Coast Railway Company, 410 U.S. 224 (1973)

Facts: Two railroad companies sued to set aside an incentive per diem rate established by the Interstate Commerce Commission in a rulemaking proceeding. For several years, the US had a shortage of freight cars to ship goods. As a result, Congress passed legislation expanding ICC's power to set per diem charges. The Commission, after an initial notice and comment period, stated that any party that wished an oral hearing shall set forth need. The Commission announced the new rate without further hearings.

Held: The Court held the actions of the ICC were proper. The Court noted that the statutory "hearing" is not the same as the "hearing on the record after notice and an opportunity to be heard." *See* APA § 556(d). The Court held that a hearing does not always encompass oral testimony and cross-examination. The ruling established that the APA does not mandate a trial-type hearing in a rulemaking proceeding when the proceeding is dealing with the interpretation of agency rules and policy. The Court held that formal written hearings are sufficient for internal rulemaking purposes.

Harry & Bryant Company v. FTC, 726 F.2d 993 (W.D. Tex.), *cert. denied* 469 U.S. 820 (1984)

Facts: The FTC investigated the funeral services industry and initiated rulemaking proceedings to regulate the industry. The FTC published notice with the proposed rule, a statement of need, and an invitation for public comment. Hearings were held, but oral testimony/cross-examination was limited so as not to take duplicative testimony. In the end, a revised rule was published. A funeral services provider who wanted to offer oral testimony was not allowed challenges.

Held: The Supreme Court held that the limitation of testimony/cross-examination was appropriate. The Court noted that the statute does not guarantee that every person is allowed to testify or cross-examine.

2. Formal Adjudications Needed

a. *Informal*

There are no formal requirements for informal adjudication under the APA. A hearing of some sort is required, but the formalities of a formal hearing need not be applied.

b. *Formal*

Formal adjudication requires all the typical formalities of a trial-type hearing: notice, representation, opening statement, witnesses, cross-examination, evidence, objections, etc.

Seacoast Anti-Pollution League v. Costle, 527 F.2d 872 (1st Cir.), *cert. denied* 439 U.S. 824 (1978)

Facts: A public utility filed for permission to release hot water from a nuclear plant into a water source by requesting a permit and the required exemption. The applicable statute provided if "after an opportunity for a public hearing" a party could "demonstrate to the satisfaction of the Administrator" that the EPA's standards are "more stringent that necessary" to protect the wildlife, the party could be allowed to meet a lower standard. A hearing was held and an administrator approved a one-time discharge. Subsequent public adjudicative hearings were held and an ALJ denied the additional permits and exemptions. The utility appealed to the Administrator, who agreed to hear the case. In the meantime a new Administrator was appointed. The new Administrator assembled a panel of advisors to assist in his technical review. The panel submitted a report finding that, with one exception, PSCO had met its burden of proof. Seacoast requested a hearing, but the Administrator denied the request. The Administrator's final decision followed the technical panel's recommendations. Seacoast appealed.

Held: The Court held that the Administrator erred in two respects: (1) by not holding a hearing to receive the responses to his request for information. The report submitted by the panel was therefore not properly part of the record. This aspect of the case was remanded for the purpose of allowing the Administrator to determine whether cross-examination would be useful; and (2) by basing his decision at least in part on the panel's report, which was not part of the record and thus an improper *ex parte* communication. This aspect of the case was also remanded so that the Administrator could remedy the error by either reaching a new decision not dependent on the panel's report or by holding a full hearing at which the panel members could be cross-examined. In sum, the court held that this was the kind of quasi-judicial proceeding for which the adjudicatory procedures of the APA were intended. The court noted that the absence of "on the record" in the statutory language regarding adjudication was not dispositive absent a congressional intent that the determination not be on the record. There was no evidence of such a congressional intent in this case. However, the key words on the record are not necessary to trigger an informal adjudication. The courts should look to the substantive nature of type of hearing that Congress intended.

Chemical Waste Management, Inc. v. EPA, 873 F.2d 1477 (D.C. Cir. 1989)
Facts: Appellant sought review of an EPA regulation that established informal administrative procedures for hearings concerning corrective action. The regulation allowed for public hearings but only insofar as revocation, suspension and penalties were concerned, and not for orders for investigation and corrective actions. With regard to the latter, EPA could use informal adjudicative procedures which included written statement, oral presentation, technical assistance, but no direct or cross- examination of witnesses. The appellant claimed that formal procedures were necessary.
Held: The court held that Congress did not set forth guidelines requiring formal procedures. The court explained that the agency provided a reasonable explanation for its choice of informal procedures, and held that the agency could operate on a reasonable interpretation of an ambiguous Congressional statute.

D. Informal Adjudications

1. Informal
The APA does not require any special procedures, only that a hearing be held (but the agency need not adhere to all the requirements of a formal hearing).

Independent U.S. Tanker Owners Committee v. Lewis, 690 F.2d 908 (1982)

Facts: This case related to the prior subsidy pay back case of the same merchant corporation. See same facts.

Held: The court proffered two reasons for reviewing an informal adjudication. First, the court is to review the record to ensure that the agency's action is not arbitrary and capricious or an abuse of discretion. (§ 706(2)(A)). Second, the court is to ensure that due process procedures are used so as to comport with the Constitution, statute, and APA. The court noted that notice, comment and response are not necessary to an informal adjudication. The agency must, however, act with enough procedures to allow meaningful judicial review, and actually follow all established procedures.

2. Policy and Informal Rule Statements

Pacific Gas & Electric Co. v. Federal Power Comm., 506 F.2d 33 (D.C. Cir. 1974)

Facts: The FPC issued a rule without holding rulemaking proceedings. The rule set forth the policy for natural gas suppliers to follow during energy shortages. The order provided that curtailment priorities would be based on use rather than on prior contractual curtailment, and listed nine categories of use. The rule also required full curtailment of lower volumes before higher volumes. A customer of the pipelines challenged this action, stating that it was rulemaking in which proper procedures were not followed (§ 553).

Held: The court held this was not rulemaking, but rather, was a statement of policy. The court noted that the agency could not rely on the statement of policy as law. A statement of policy announces the direction that the agency intends to take in the future. The agency still must initiate formal rulemaking proceedings, and at that time the appellants may have their say.

E. Decision: Rulemaking or Adjudication

1. Choices

For most federal agencies, there is a choice between substantive rulemaking involving APA § 553 or adjudication involving APA §§ 554, 556, and 557. Unless mandated by statute, the agency is normally free to choose which method to employ in what context.

2. Cases

SEC v. Chenery I, 318 U.S. 80 (1943)

Facts: Insiders in a public utility undergoing reorganization attempted to capitalize on the situation by acquiring additional stock in the company on the open market. The SEC ruled this "unfair," and refused to approve the plan.

Held: The Supreme Court reviewed the ruling, and held that courts may only review agency decisions based on the proffered reasoning for acting. The Court held that the reasons that SEC gave were not sufficient to support its actions. The Court remanded to the commission. On remand, the SEC reexamined the problem, recast its rationale and reached the same result.

SEC v. Chenery II, 332 U.S. 194 (1947)

Facts: The facts are the same as *SEC v. Chenery I*, except the SEC held a rulemaking hearing. The statute also allowed the SEC to conduct a hearing to determine whether the voluntary proposal was necessary to effectuate the provisions of the reorganization. The result was that the SEC denounced the voluntary plan in a formal rulemaking session. The Chenery plan was therefore denied once again.

Held: The Supreme Court held that the agency action was proper because procedures were followed. There was no abuse of discretion by the Commission.

Bell Aerospace v. NLRB, 475 F.2d 485 (2nd Cir. 1973)

Facts: Bell refused to bargain with the buyers at one of its facilities, saying they were beyond the reach of the NLRB. The NLRB concluded that the buyers could unionize. Bell countered that the NLRB decision was incorrect in two respects. First, the Board had changed its original stance excluding all managerial employees, now excluding only some managerial employees. Second, even if some managerial employees are exempt from the exclusion, Bell argued the buyer was not one of them.

Held: Regarding the first argument, the court concluded that the NLRB could not reinterpret the Act whenever they so chose. However, the court noted that the NLRB could, after the proper adjudicatory proceedings, conclude that buyers are not managerial employees as contemplated by the statute.

F. Rules and Retroactivity

1. Separation of Rulemaking and Adjudication

Bowen v. Georgetown Hospital, 488 U.S. 204 (1988)

Facts: The government allowed reimbursement to health care providers for costs incurred in treating Medicare patients. The enabling act allowed the Secretary of Health and Human Services (HHS) to promulgate regulations regarding calculation on costs. HHS changed the calculations, whereupon various medical providers challenged the calculation schedule, alleging the HHS should have performed formal notice-and-comment rulemaking. HHS paid on the old schedule and instituted rulemaking proceedings regarding the new calculations. Two years later, Congress passed legislation favoring the Secretary's standards. A retroactive cost-limit rule was then implemented to recoup costs.

Held: The Supreme Court announced that retroactive legislation is not favored by the law. While courts and Congress have the power to apply decisions retroactively, agencies have no such power of retroactivity. The Court held that the APA was designed to be prospective only, not retroactive.

2. Hearings and Rules

Heckler v. Campbell, 461 U.S. 458 (1983)

Facts: The Social Security Act defined and set criteria for disability. HHS adopted the definition. Previously, in applying the statute, the HHS first made a determination as to the availability of suitable jobs, and second, as to the qualifications (for any such jobs) of the claimant. This led to uneven treatment of claimants. HHS responded by adopting medical-vocational guidelines, which called for an evaluation of four factors: physical ability, age, education, and work experience. If, after consideration of such factors, suitable employment existed no disability benefits would be given. A claimant applied for disability benefits relating to a back injury. The ALJ decided that the claimant could no longer perform her current job duties but was still employable in other capacities. The claimant raised a due process challenge.

Held: The Supreme Court held that due process was not violated. The Court noted that guidelines are not like rules in that they still have the power to adapt to an individual, whereas a rule is not adaptable to an individual. The decision afforded adaptability without the need for rulemaking for each possible set of circumstances.

G. Agency Action and Private Citizens

1. Participation of Community

Office of Comm. Of United Church of Christ v. FCC, 359 F.2d 994 (1966)

Facts: The appeal was the result of the FCC's decision to renew a TV station's license for one year. The appellants sought to oppose the license but their claim was dismissed by the FCC without a hearing. The appellants alleged that the TV station discriminated based on racial and religious grounds, and filed the petition on behalf of "all the television viewers in the State of Mississippi." The FCC traditionally granted standing only to persons who were electronics manufacturers and are in competition with the TV station.

Held: The court held that while there is a presumption that agency action is in the best interest of the public, the FCC's failure to follow up on complaints invalidated that presumption. Furthermore, it was the appellant who asserted issues and objections in the public interest. The court held that the agency has control of its own proceedings, but warned that standing is a judicial concept, not to be determined at the whim of an agency.

Heckler v. Chaney, 470 U.S. 821 (1985)

Facts: The respondents were death row inmates who petitioned the FDA, complaining that the drugs used for lethal injection were not regulated by the government. The inmates alleged that the drugs were administered by untrained professionals, and as a result the intended effect of a quick and painless death was not achieved. The FDA declined to investigate. The Court of Appeals held that an agency's failure to act is reviewable in a court.

Held: The Supreme Court held that failure to act can be reviewed in certain circumstances, but not in the case at bar. The Court reviewed APA §§ 701-706 and found that judicial review is not possible when (1) preempted by statute, or (2) the proposed action is in the complete discretion of the agency. The Court held that judicial review is presumptively unavailable in cases of agency inaction, but that the presumption is rebuttable by a showing that statutory guidelines were not followed. .

2. Media

Agencies may place limits -- but not wholesale exclusion -- on the attendance of family members and friends at agency proceedings. While the Supreme Court has never ruled on the First Amendment right of the media to attend agency matters, conventional wisdom is that the media does have a right to attend, but that it may be limited just as in the judicial system.

IV. JUDICIAL REVIEW

This section covers judicial intervention, and examines when and how courts may review agency decisions, and to what extent. This section delineates the standards courts must utilize when reviewing agency's actions and discusses the remedies available when a court deems them appropriate.

A. Questions of Fact

1. APA § 706

This section governs questions of fact. The court has the power to hold an agency action unlawful and set it aside. In doing, so, however, a court must find that the action was either:

a. Arbitrary & capricious or an abuse of discretion;
b. Beyond the power authorized by statute;
c. Unconstitutional;
d. Unsupported by substantial evidence; or
e. Committed without following agency procedures

Note: APA does not apply to judicial review of Patent Office's factual determination. In Re Zurko (Fed. Cir. 1998) (en banc Federal Circuit unanimously held that that "clear error" standard should be used instead of the APA's "arbitrary, capricious, or abuse of discretion" standard. The United States Supreme Court affirmed this decision in Dickinson v. Zurko, 119 S. Ct. 1916 (1999), supra.

---

2. How much Supporting Evidence?

a. Substantial Evidence; More than Scintilla

Universal Camera Corporation v. NLRB, 340 U.S. 474 (1951)
Facts: A supervisor testified on behalf of labor at an NLRB hearing. Subsequently, the same supervisor was fired – ostensibly, for being drunk on duty. An issue existed as to the reason for his firing. The Board held for the supervisor. The case came before the Supreme Court because of a disagreement in the Circuit Courts as to the effect of the newly enacted APA and Taft-Hartley Acts on the duties of courts when called upon to review orders of the NLRB.

Held: The Supreme Court vacated and remanded. The Court noted that a reviewing court does not serve in its usual judicial function when reviewing an agency action. The Court held that the Board's decision will generally be respected. However, after a review of the record the court may set it aside based on "a fair estimate of the worth of the testimony of witnesses or its informed judgment." In essence, the Court developed a test which asked whether there was substantial evidence to support the agency's findings. The Court held "substantial evidence" must be more than a scintilla; it is the amount of evidence necessary for a reasonable person to be drawn to the same conclusion. The Court articulated that it is up to the Court of Appeals to decide whether the Board's decision was based upon "substantial evidence". Since there was no such finding, the Court remanded.

Dickinson Acting Commissioner of Patents and Trademarks v. Zurko, No. 98-377 (June 10, 1999)
Facts: The PTO denied a patent after reviewing respondent's application for the same. The respondent sued and the Federal Circuit reversed. The Federal Circuit used the review of "clearly erroneous".
Held: The Court held that the PTO must use the framework devised by § 706 when reviewing an agency's findings of fact. The Court held that a reviewing court must use the less stringent "arbitrary and capricious standard" of the APA when reviewing an agency's decision, rather than the more stringent court-to-court review of "clearly erroneous." The Court reversed and remanded.

b. *Substantial Evidence*

    i. Substantial evidence is the amount a reasonable person would need to accept the conclusion based on the evidence.

    ii. Only the Court of Appeals, as the first tier of judicial review, can determine whether there was "substantial evidence."

Association of Data Processing Services Organizations, Inc. v. Board of Governors of the Federal Reserve, 745 F.2d 677 (D.C. Cir. 1984)

Facts: ADPSO, a trade organization, filed a petition for review of an FRB decision relating to the ability of banks to establish data processing services. The Bank Holding Companies Act of 1956 required banks seeking to engage in non-banking activities to gain prior regulatory approval. The act required review of the Board's facts to be conducted in light of the substantial evidence standard The Board held for the banks after hearings. ADPSO sought a higher standard of review. The bank contended that the standard should be "arbitrary and capricious."

Held: The court held the last line of the Act's section as controlling: "on the record." The court interpreted this to mean the standard is "arbitrary and capricious," "supported by substantial evidence."

3. Role of Administrative Law Judges

Penasquitos Village, Inc. v. NLRB, 565 F.2d 1074 (9th Cir. 1977)

Issue: The question concerned the relative weights must a court was to afford the findings of an agency and an ALJ in instances where two differed.

Held: The court held the Board was not bound by the ALJ's credibility determinations, but that ALJ's determinations carry a lot of weight. A reviewing court must review a reversal of ALJ by the Board more critically if the Board's findings differ from the ALJ's findings. The court noted that trial determinations (trial demeanor, actions in the court) fall strongly in the favor of the ALJ, whereas there is more leeway to the agency regarding changes in factual determinations.

B. Review of Law/Policy - Traditional Approach

1. Application of Law to the Facts

O'Leary v. Brown-Pacific Maxon Inc., 340 U.S. 504 (1951)

Facts: The Appellant employer maintained a recreation area near a shoreline for its employees. The water was dangerous and swimming was prohibited. An employee at the recreation centerheard cries for help from the water and, along with approximately 20 other employees plunged into the water to help. The employee drowned and his mother filed a worker's compensation claim. The agency ordered death benefits and the appellant contested. The ALJ noted that all that was required was "that the obligations or conditions of employment create the zone of special danger out of which the injury arose." The district court upheld the determination, but was reversed by the Court of Appeals. The Supreme Court granted certiorari.

Held: The Supreme Court reversed and ordered reinstatement of the death benefits. The Court held that the findings must be upheld unless they are unsupported by substantial evidence on the record.

2. Application of the Facts to the Law

NLRB v. Hearst Publishing Corp., 322 U.S. 111 (1944)

Facts: Newsboys attempted to unionize for the purpose of negotiating a collective bargaining agreement. The company refused to negotiate, claiming the law did not apply to newsboys, who worked various degrees of full time, part time, temporary, sporadic and seasonal employment. The NLRB held that the newsboys could unionize and that Hearst's refusal was an unfair labor practice.

Held: The Supreme Court noted the difference between employees and independent contractors and turned to legislative history for the answer. The Court held that Congress had intended the prevalent master-servant relationship to be employer-employee. The Court, in reversing the NLRB decision, held that the newsboys did not have this type of relationship with Hearst. The Court noted that uniformity of the law was an issue, and that in order to have uniformity as intended by Congress, it was up to the NLRB to make a determination to prevent different standards from court to court (state to state). The Court's test was to look at the legislative history of the statute to make a determination. An agency determination as to the applicability of a broad statutory term will be granted deference if it has "warrant in the record" and a reasonable basis in the law.

Packard Motor Car Co. v. NLRB, 330 U.S. 485 (1947)
Issue: (Considered with the previous case.) The question was whether a foreman could organize for collective bargaining under the NLRA. "Employees" were defined as persons acting in the interest of an employer, indirectly or directly.
Held: The Court affirmed the NLRB determination. However, the Court made an independent review with no deference to the NLRB. This case (Supreme Court reasoning) was overruled by the Taft-Hartley Act.

Skidmore v. Swift & Co., 323 U.S. 134 (1944)
Facts: Seven employees of a fire hall brought an action under the Fair Labor Standards Act. The firefighters were required to stay at the fire hall or be within hailing distance for several days at a time and were paid a fixed amount plus an additional sum if there was a fire call. The firefighters claimed they were entitled to overtime for their waiting time. The District Court, affirmed by the Court of Appeals, held as a matter of law that waiting time is never work time.
Held: The Supreme Court reversed. The Court found that waiting time was compensable in this situation. The Court noted that neither the statute nor case law precludes the consideration of waiting time as work time. The "waiting as work time" issue was deemed a question of fact; therefore, the case was remanded. The Court held that an agency's actions are not controlling but persuasive.

C. Modern Approach

1. Law and Politics

Citizens to Preserve Overton Park, Inc. v. Volpe, 401 U.S. 402 (1971)

Facts: The Department of Transportation decided to build a highway through Overton Park. DOT claimed that it was the only viable route and therefore was allowable under the parkland preservation statute. The Secretary of the DOT approved the route without publishing or otherwise offering any findings of fact. The appellant organization sued to enjoin construction, arguing the Secretary failed to make his own findings of fact and relied solely on the findings of the city council.

Held: Judicial Review is presumptively available here, and while formal findings are unnecessary, judicial review based only on litigation affidavits is inadequate. "Substantial evidence" burden is not applicable if it wasn't APA "rulemaking". *De novo* review is not available if it was neither adjudicatory action with inadequate fact-finding, nor a case of new issues raised in the enforcement of non-adjudicatory action. The Court used the "substantial inquiry" test and remanded for consideration of the full administrative record.

2. Discretion in Informal Adjudications

Camp v. Pitts, 411 U.S. 138 (1973)

Facts: Without a hearing or published findings, the Comptroller of Currency denied an application to organize a new bank. The decision was published in the form of a letter. The applicant sued, and summary judgment was granted by the trial court for the Comptroller. The Court of Appeals reversed and ordered a *de novo* trial.

Held: The Supreme Court reversed. The Court held *de novo* review is only appropriate when the fact finding procedures are inadequate. The Court reiterated that Overton Park requires the reviewing court to determine whether the agency action was "arbitrary and capricious" or abuse of discretion. If the court finds a deficiency under one of these standards, then the proper action is to reverse and remand, not to hold a *de novo* trial.

3. Informal Rulemaking - Arbitrary & Capricious

***Motor Vehicle Manufacturers Association of the U.S., Inc. v. State
Farm Mutual Mobile Insurance Co.,*** 463 U.S. 29 (1983)

Facts: Congress passed the Motor Vehicle Safety Act of 1966 in an
attempt to reduce the number of motor vehicle deaths. The statute
directed the Secretary of Transportation to promulgate safety rules.
The act stated that the Secretary must consider all relevant safety
data and consider the reasonableness and practicability for motor
vehicles. The act also called for judicial review, per APA §706, for
any standard that is revoked. Without explanation, the NHTSA
rescinded its passive restraint requirement.

Held: The Supreme Court held the agency must provide a
reasonable explanation and analysis for a revocationAn agency
changing its course by rescinding a rule is obligated to supply a
reasoned analysis for the change – sometimes even beyond that
which was required when an agency does not act at all.

Allentown Mack Sales & Service, Inc. v. National Labor and Relations Board, No. 96-795 (January 26, 1998).

Facts: Mack Trucks ("Mack") sold its Allentown, PA branch to Allentown Mack Sales Inc. ("Allentown") and retained several of the original employees. Mack's branches service and parts employees were represented by Local Lodge 724 of the machinist union, and a number of themstated that the union had lost their support. Allentown, an independent dealership, refused Local Lodge 724's request for commencement of collective-bargaining negotiations, claiming a good-faith, reasonable doubt as to the union's support by the new mix of employees. Allentown arranged a poll of the employees who voted 19 to 13 against the union. The union then filed suit charging violations of the unfair labor practices. NLRB precedent held that an employer who entertained a good faith reasonable doubt whether a majority of its employees supports the current union had three options: (1) request a formal Board certification, (2) withdraw recognition of the union and support, or (3) conduct an informal poll of employee support for the union. The ALJ held against Allentown, citing Allentown's lack of anobjective reasonable doubt about the majority status of union supporters, ordered Allentown to recognize and bargain with the union. The Court of Appeals enforced the order.

Held: The Supreme Court reversed and remanded. The Court held the NLRB rule that allows an employer to sever ties with the union is irrational, but that it is not arbitrary or capricious under the APA. The Court went on to deal with the three methods of the NLRB allowance of union tie severance. The Court opined that a reasonable jury could not have found that Allentown lacked a good faith reasonable doubt about the union support. The Court held although the standard was irrational it was not in violation of the APA, and that Allentown's informal poll met the criteria eschew recognition of the union's right to represent the employees.

D. Judicial Review: ALJ Discretion and the Law

Chevron U.S.A., Inc. v. NRDC, 467 U.S. 837, *rehearing_denied* 468 U.S. 1227 (1984)

Facts: Under a permit system set up by the EPA to enforce the provisions of the Clean Air Act, compliance was attained by the creation of "bubbles" within which pollutants were released. In their efforts to comply with the regulations, polluters were allotted a set amount of pollution. Facilities could modify their method of compliance. A question arose as to whether the system was a maintenance of current air quality or whether it improved air quality as mandated by the Clean Air Act. The Court of Appeals disapproved of the agency's interpretation of "stationary source" under the statute.

Held: The Supreme Court reversed. The Court noted that the agency is the entity with the expertise to balance policy objectives set forth by Congress. The Court set forth two steps for courts to follow: (1) Did Congress speak to the issue directly? If yes, defer to the Congressional language. (2) If statute is silent or ambiguous then defer to the agency if the agency reasonably interprets the statute. The Court did not look at legislative history for its determination. The Court held the bubble regulation is reasonable in light of policy for clean air vs. industry growth. The Court may challenge whether an agency interpretation within a gap left by Congress is reasonable, but it may not challenge the wisdom of the agency's policy.

Note: This case is in opposition to *Hearst* but *Hearst* was never overruled. It depends upon the reviewing court as to which standard is utilized.

Chevron Test Applied

MCI v. AT&T, 114 S. Ct. 2223 (1994)

Facts: The Communications Act of 1934 required long distance carriers to file their tariffs with the FCC and to charge only the filed rates. At the time, the only true long distance carrier was AT&T. The statute allowed "modification" of any requirement. With the increase of long distance carriers in the late 1970's, the FCC relaxed the filing requirements for everyone except AT&T. In 1992, following rulemaking hearings, the FCC declared the filing of tariffs optional for all "non-dominant carriers." The issue was whether the FCC's act was a modification or deletion of an existing requirement. The D.C. Circuit said that the action was not authorized by the statute.

Held: The Supreme Court affirmed. The Court called this the "battle of the dictionaries," regarding the definition of the term "modification." The Court ruled "modification" was a slight change whereas a deletion was a substantial change, and held that the FCC's action was a deletion.

U.S. v. Haggar Apparel Co., No. 97-2044 (April 21, 1999)
Facts: Haggar Apparel sent fabrics made in the US to plants in Mexico for assembly. Haggar would then sell the resulting clothing to its customers in the US. The US imposed full tariffs on the clothes returning from Mexico. The Harmonized Tariff Schedule of the U.S. (HTSUS) allowed for a partial duty exemption if the articles were only assembled and not otherwise improved. In Mexico, Haggar permapressed the garments, i.e., baking garments with chemicals, in "order to maintain their creases and avoid wrinkles." The US claimed that this was an "improvement" and therefore no partial duty exemption was authorized. Haggar sued in the Court of International Trade, which held that the partial exemption was allowable. The Court of Appeals affirmed refusing to analyze the regulation under Chevron.
Held: The Supreme Court vacated and remanded. The Court held that the regulation was subject to Chevron analysis.

Immigration and Naturalization Service v. Aguirre-Aguirre, 119 S. Ct. 1439 (1999).
Facts: The Immigration and Nationality Act stated that a person was entitled to stop deportation if they demonstrated that it was more likely than not that they would be subject to persecution because of race, religion, nationality, or membership in a particular social group or political opinion. However, if the Attorney General determined that the person had committed a "serious nonpolitical crime" outside the United States prior to their arrival, they could nevertheless be deported. Aguirre-Aguirre in protest of high bus fares, had assisted in the burning of several buses prior to his arrival in the U.S. The AG held this to be a serious nonpolitical crime and continued with the deportation. The Ninth Circuit stopped deportation and opined that the INS/BIA should weigh additional factors.
Held: A unanimous Supreme Court reversed the Ninth Circuit. The Court held that Chevron should be used to analyze the case, and that the proper inquiry was whether the statute was ambiguous as to the meaning of a statutory term and if the agency's interpretation of the term was reasonable.

FDA v. Brown & Williamson Tobacco Corp., No. 98-1152 (March 21, 2000).
Facts: 21 U.S.C. § 301 (Food, Drug and Cosmetic Act - FDCA) gave the FDA, as the designee of the Secretary of Health and Human Services, the right to regulate "drugs" and "devices." The FDA used this statute to regulate tobacco products, rationalizing that nicotine was a drug and that cigarettes and smokeless tobacco constituted devices. The FDA promulgated regulations regarding the product's promotion, labeling and accessibility to children. The FDA's findings in support of the regulation included health risks to adults and children. Several tobacco related manufacturers and retailers sued. The District Court upheld the FDA's right to regulate the tobacco industry. The Fifth Circuit reversed.
Held: The Supreme Court upheld the Fifth Circuit. The Court noted that the FDCA, especially in light of congressional action in tobacco-specific regulation, did not give the FDA the authority to regulate promotion of tobacco products. The Court used the Chevron test, and held that in reading the FDCA, Congress did not intend to give the FDA the regulatory power. The Court noted that if the tobacco products were under their jurisdiction (because of the FDA's finding of serious health effect) the FDA would have to remove all the products from the shelf as the FDCA allowed only safe products to be on the shelf.

Christensen v. Harris County, No. 98-1176 (May 1, 2000).
Facts: 29 U.S.C. § 201 (Fair Labor Standards Act, FLSA) permitted states and their divisions to compensate employees for overtime work via compensatory time instead of cash. If an employee did not use compensatory time, then the employer was required to pay overtime. Harris County, fearing the costs of paying of cash to its employees, mandated that all employees schedule compensatory time earned. The employees sued. The District Court held that the policy violated the FLSA. The Fifth Circuit reversed, stating that the FLSA was silent therefore deference must be given to the county policy.
Held: The Supreme Court affirmed. The court held that nothing in the FLSA or its regulations prohibited a public employer from compelling the use of compensatory time.

E. Agency Appeal

Once the ALJ renders a decision, there is usually an agency appeal process that takes place prior to a final decision. The appeal tribunal will usually assume that the ALJ decision is correct; the appealing party therefore bears the burdens of persuasion and proof. *See* Fukuda v. City of Angels, 20 Cal.4th 805 (1999).

Hearne v. Sherman, 1999 N.C. Lexis 720, 1999 WL 528170 (1999).
Facts: Hearne was released from his duties as an animal control officer. The question was whether Hearne voluntarily resigned as the animal control officer or, as Hearne asserted, was fired wrongfully. An independent ALJ ruled Hearne had not voluntarily resigned and had not been discharged for good cause. The State Personnel Commission agreed with the ALJs decision. However, Sherman, the agency head (who had been involved in Hearne's case) ruled that the resignation was voluntary. Writing in his opinion that, "It is evident that either Mr. Sherman or Mr. Hearne is lying about certain points," Sherman held himself credible and Hearne untruthful.
Held: The North Carolina Supreme Court upheld Sherman's determination that he was telling the truth, his findings on the credibility issue, and the maintenance of Hearst's due process rights.

V. CONSTITUTIONAL ISSUES IN ADMINISTRATIVE LAW

This section covers the various constitutional issues involved in administrative law. It discusses when a constitutional issue is a factor and when it is not, reviews when and what types of procedures are mandated when dealing with an agency issue, and reviews what constitutes a "property" and "liberty" interest when dealing with administrative issues.

A. Procedural Due Process

1. In General

Joint Anti-Fascist Refugee League v. McGrath, 341 U.S. 123 (1951)

Facts: The US Attorney General was granted the power to place a person or group on a list of individuals suspected of not being loyal to the US government. The list was distributed and utilized in hiring, firing, and promotions within the federal government. Three alleged Communist organizations were placed on this list, resulting in their membership being the organizations that were sued.

Held: The Supreme Court held that the result of this list was to remove the targeted individuals from their government jobs. The Court held that the jobs were a property interest and any deprivation must comport with due process. Due process safeguards were necessary prior to placement on the list. The Court held that the same standard applied to agencies. The Court noted a balancing test had to be utilized in deciding the type of process. The factors include the nature of the interest, manner of action, reasons for action, availability of alternative procedures, and protection needed with regard to the interest.

    a. **Balancing Test of the following factors**:
        i. Nature of interest which is affected;
        ii. How it was affected;
        iii. Government interest;
        iv. Reasonable alternatives;
        v. Degree and nature of interest affected vs. goal to be achieved.

    b. **Applies to Rulemaking and Adjudications**

Goldberg v. Kelly, 397 U.S. 254 (1970)

Facts: . Welfare benefits were terminated without a prior hearing. The question for the Court was whether a state must supply an evidentiary hearing prior to the termination of the benefits.

Held: The Court held that where the benefits are in place, a full adversarial pre-termination evidentiary hearing is required before termination of welfare benefits. These benefits are a special case in that they often provide the means of subsistence and therefore must not be incorrectly suspended pending resolution. The Court said a written evidentiary hearing was not feasible here because many such claimants are illiterate, and posited that an oral argument could better be molded to the situation.

2. Modern Interpretation

Board of Regents of State Colleges v. Roth, 408 U.S. 564 (1972)

Facts: The college hired a teacher for a one-year term. The teacher was informed that he would not be rehired for the next academic year. The teacher had no tenure rights to continued employment. The teacher was given no reason for the non-retention and no opportunity to challenge it at any sort of hearing.

The District Court, affirmed by the Court of Appeals, found for the teacher on the procedural issues.

Held: The Supreme Court reversed, holding that due process was not violated. The Court noted that a reason for the non-renewal was not necessary. The teacher was not tenured. Due process procedural requirements apply only to the deprivation of interests encompassed by the 14th Amendment's protection of "liberty" and "property". Here, the Court articulated that the old contract had expired and a new one had never been granted, therefore the teacher had no constitutionally protected interest of which he could be deprived.

Perry v. Sindermann, 408 U.S. 593 (1972)

Facts: This was a companion case to *Roth.* The Appellant worked for the Texas school system for several years, the last four at a particular school. The contracts were each one year contracts. Because of his election as president to a local teacher's association and subsequent criticisms of the school system, his contract was not renewed. He was given no reason and no hearing.

Held: The Supreme Court noted that while the teacher had no explicit contractual claim of tenure, there were free speech issues and a *de facto* tenure system rendering summary judgment inappropriate. State law stated that a teacher could acquire tenure after four consecutive one-year contracts, after which the teacher could only be removed for good cause. The teacher had to be given an opportunity to prove the legitimacy of his claim to the entitlement of reemployment. If he succeeds therein, he was owed a hearing.

Meachum v. Fano, 427 U.S. 215 (1976)

Facts: The question presented was whether due process mandates that a prisoner be given a hearing prior to his transfer to a prison where conditions were less favorable. State law was silent on the point. Respondents set several fires at a prison. Individual classification hearings were held at which they were represented by counsel. The hearing consisted of the reading of a prepared statement of the Board, the Board listening to a superintendent's testimony in camera, and the respondents being told of the allegations against them. Each respondent was allowed to present evidence. The Board recommended transfer to stricter prisons; however, none of the prisoners were disciplined in any fashion. The District Court reversed the Board, ordering a hearing, and was affirmed by the Court of Appeals.

Held: The Supreme Court reversed and held no hearing was necessary. The Court rejected the notion that any grievous loss by a person at the hands of the State automatically demands procedural due process. In this case, due process protects a person in the first instance from unlawful/unconstitutional convictions. Those due process rights were followed and the respondents were convicted. Once convicted a prisoner has been constitutionally deprived of some of his former rights. Confinement can then take place in any manner which does not violate the Constitution. There is no state law which grants a prisoner a property or liberty interest in remaining in a certain prison facility.

3. **Court Determination of Whether there was Adequate Protection of Due Process Rights**

Mathews v. Eldridge, 424 U.S. 319 (1976)

Facts: The issue presented in this case was whether due process mandates an evidentiary hearing prior to the termination of Social Security disability benefits.

Held: The Supreme Court concluded that a prior evidentiary hearing was not necessary. The Court utilized a three-part test. First, the court must look to the private interest that will be affected by the agency action. Second, the court must evaluate the risk of erroneous deprivation of the interest through the procedures utilized, and the value and feasibility of any alternative procedures. Third, the court must examine the fiscal and administrative burdens to the government. Here, the Court held that the interest was not as significant as the one in *Goldberg v. Kelly*.

Ingraham v. Wright, 430 U.S. 651 (1977)

Facts: The issue was whether a prior hearing was necessary before a school could utilize corporal punishment. Eighth and ninth graders sued Dade County, Florida school officials. The paddling consisted of a student bending over while an official used a two foot long, three inch wide, and two inch thick board and swatted four to five times on the buttocks. A certain student received 20 swats in the principal's office.

Held: The Supreme Court used the above three-part test. The Court held the Eighth Amendment did not apply to the paddling of children. The Court held there is a liberty interest in not being paddled, however, the procedures and common law remedies provided adequate protection. The Court noted if the paddling was too severe to match the "crime" then the child/parent could seek damages in court.

Dissent: Minority said that the common law remedies were available too late. The liberty interest would have already been violated unconstitutionally. Procedures for additional safeguards would not destroy the system.

4. State Action Doctrine

Note: Only the Government must provide due process; there is no requirement that the private sector provide due process. For that reason, courts only review arbitrary decisions by governments or their agents. See Lebron v. National RR Passenger Corp., 5113 U.S. 374 (1995).

VI.   ADMINISTRATIVE PROCESS

This section deals with the process of administrative law. Previously, we discussed formal and informal adjudication, and formal and informal rulemaking. This section explains when each is appropriate, and further explains the process of each method, and the effect it has on the parties, the agency and the public. This section concludes with a discussion on *ex parte* contact.

A.   Agency Decisions

1.   Administrative Law Judges (ALJ)
Administrative law Judges are the first line in the adjudication process. They are independent from the enforcement section of the agency. However, they do answer to the same authority as the rest of the agency.

2.   Proceedings
The ALJ must hold a trial-type hearing that is "on the record." This means a record must be kept of the proceeding in case of appeal to a higher authority.

Morgan v. United States I, 298 U.S. 468 (1936)
Facts: Pre-APA case. Fifty suits were consolidated for trial. The suit sought to restrain the Secretary of Agriculture from fixing the maximum rate to be charged by market agencies for buying and selling livestock. There was no hearing other than a ruling by an ALJ on the proposed Order. The statute called for a full hearing. The individuals alleged that this required individual hearings.
Held: The Supreme Court struck the Order. The Court said that this was not a full hearing. The Court noted that the Secretary can not just rely on staff and research, but that briefs and non-agency evidence must be considered as well. The Court held that the agency must look at all the information submitted regardless of the amount of work it takes. The agency must also make a report or brief of its contentions so that the other party may have a chance to know and respond to those contentions. If the statute delegates the authority to a person, the person can not further delegate that authority. The Court also held that the same person who performs the fact-finding must hear the case.

Morgan v. United States II, 304 U.S. 1 (1938)
Facts: Same facts, Solicitor General petitioned for rehearing.
Held: The Supreme Court denied the petition, holding there was no inconsistency with their earlier ruling that an examiner's report may not always be required when the Secretary himself makes the findings. Here, the Secretary made the findings based on an *ex parte* discussion with the active prosecutors without affording the other party knowledge of the claims presented.

3. Separation of Functions within the Agency In General

    a.   There must be separate and distinct departments within the agency for the decision makers and the judges.

    b.   The "prosecutors" of the agency cannot be aligned with the judges without violating due process.

    c.   The judge should have no interest in the outcome of, or prior involvement in the case, subject to the Doctrine of Necessity.

    d.   Doctrine of Necessity. This doctrine holds that a judge should not be involved in a case in which he/she has a personal interest unless the judge is absolutely the only person available to hold the hearing. In any event, the judge should disclose details of any relevant involvement on the record.

    e.   The separation of functions doctrine does not apply to informal rulemaking.

AT&T, 60 FCC 1 (1976)
Facts: The FCC considered changing AT&T rates for certain commercial telephone services. A trial was held and an order was forthcoming to that effect. Common Carrier Bureau represented the FCC before the ALJ. The Common Carrier Bureau filed a recommended decision with the FCC; the respondent claimed this action was inappropriate.
Held: The court held that the CCB was still fair and impartial, and that the recommendation was allowable. The court stated the agency may consider any information available from whatever source. Separation of functions is not an absolute and strict doctrine in agency law.

B. Formal Adjudications and the Agency

1. Role of the ALJ

a. Just as in the judicial system, the ALJ is to be an unbiased adjudicator, even though he/she is under the auspices of the agency.

b. The ALJ is presumed to act in good faith, follow the law, and ignore outside influence, including the agency's desired outcome.

Withrow v. Larkin, 421 U.S. 35 (1975)
Facts: Prior to Roe, the respondent doctor was performing abortions. The State Medical Board conducted a closed hearing with the respondent and his attorney. The Board charged the respondent with practicing under an assumed name and several other professional violations. The Board sought to revoke the respondent's license. In the meantime, the respondent had gone to court and received an injunction to stop the Board from acting. The respondent argued the enabling statute was unconstitutional in allowing the same Board to investigate and then adjudicate.
Held: The Supreme Court held that the dual purpose of the Board was constitutional. The Court noted that agencies are presumed to be honest and unbiased in their investigations and adjudications. The burden is on the respondent to prove bias in order to maintain such an action.

2. Ex Parte Contact

a. *Ex Parte* Contact
An ex parte contact is any oral or written communication between the ALJ and only one party to the action, or other biased entity, not on the record.

b. Party/Interested Party
The contact does not necessarily have to be with an actual participant. For example, the ALJ talking to the father of a party to a hearing about the case would be an *ex parte* contact.

c. *Ex Parte* Not Allowed
Ex parte contact is unacceptable behavior by the ALJ and is grounds for dismissal/disbarment for both the ALJ and the contacting person (if an attorney). Any

contact must be on the record with reasonable advanced notice to the other party. Contact is permissible with one side if the other side receives notice and waives or acquiesces, but the contact must be on the record.

Professional Air Traffic Controllers Org. v. FLRA, 685 F.2d 547 (D.C. Cir. 1982)
Facts: Congress passed a statute which prohibited air traffic controllers from striking. Subsequently, the controllers went on strike in violation of the statute. PATCO was the union that represented the controllers. At a hearing, the ALJ Board stripped PATCO of union certification. There were allegations of improper *ex parte* contacts. One ALJ Board member talked to FLRA General Counsel. In another instance, the Secretary of Labor contacted the judges, and as a result, a judge met with union sympathizers. After the fact, the Justice Department investigated.
Held: The court analyzed each of the contacts. The court held that the contact with the general counsel's office was allowable. The court found that even though the case was discussed, the merits of the case were not. The court turned to the Secretary's contact and held there was no violation. The court noted the conversation dealt with the filing and expediency of the case, not with the merits. The court turned to a judge's dinner with the union members, one of whom was a friend of the judge. During dinner he emphasized that revocation of the certification would destroy the union. The judge ultimately voted for revocation. The court looked to § 557(d). The section prohibited *ex parte* contact on the merits of the case. The court upheld the order. The court stated that with regard to *ex parte* contact – the court must look at: (1) the gravity of the *ex parte* contact; (2) whether the contact influenced a decision; (3) whether the party making the contact benefited from the agency's decision; (4) whether the opposing party had an opportunity to respond; and (5) whether vacating and remanding would serve a purpose.

3. Congressional Involvement

Pillsbury Co. v. FTC, 354 F.2d 952 (5th Cir. 1966)
Facts: The FTC filed a complaint against Pillsbury challenging their decision to buy four competing flour mills in one area. The examiner dismissed the complaint. The FTC reinstated it on appeal and remanded. The Commissioner adopted a rule saying that even if

competition had been diminished, the FTC had the initial adjudicatory burden. On remand Congressional antitrust subcommittee members talked to the FTC Chairman before the committee. The committee was upset that a per se rule was not utilized. One committee member extensively questioned the ongoing Pillsbury hearings. The FTC chairman recused himself from any participation in the Pillsbury case. Five years later, the FTC ordered Pillsbury to divest itself and restore the competition. The FTC chairman had already resigned. Pillsbury appealed.

Held: The court held that the Congressional interference was not improper because all of the influenced persons had left the agency prior to the decision. The court intimated that had any of the influenced persons remained, the result may have been different. The Court noted that Congress did not intervene in its legislative capacity but, rather, in a judicial function. The appeal was vacated and the case remanded to the FTC.

4. Presidential Involvement

    a.   If the action by the agency is judicial in nature, then no *ex parte* contact is allowed.

    b.   If the action by the agency is rulemaking, then contact is allowed.

Sierra Club v. Costle, 657 F.2d 298 (D.C. Cir. 1981)

Facts: The EPA issued a revised source performance standard for air quality. The coal industry was severely affected and fought the rule. Senator Byrd (WV) stated he would only vote for SALT (another statute important to the President) if the EPA would reverse the rule. After *ex parte* pressure from the President, and an "*ex parte* blitz" by industry after the close of the comment period, the EPA reversed. An environmental group sued under the CAA saying that the only information which could properly be considered is that which was on the record.

Held: The court held there was no procedural error. The President is the chief of the executive branch. Most actions by him regarding the agencies under his control are internal policing. Presidential influence is a matter of internal reasoning and decision-making within the agency. Second, Congressional meetings were held not to influence but to see how Congress might confront the issue. Third, most of the contacts were placed in the record before promulgation of the lower standards, and comment was allowed. Those that came too late were found not to be of vital importance.

c. **Test from *Costle***
Two conditions must be met before an agency rule may be reversed because of improper congressional pressure:

    i.   The content of the pressure is to make the decision-maker utilize factors not treated or mandated in the statute; and

    ii. The decision by the decision-maker must use those factors in their determination.

5. Communication not on the Record

HBO v. FCC, 567 F.2d 9, *cert. denied* 434 U.S. 829 (C.A.D.C. 1977)
Facts: The FCC brought a three year notice and comment rulemaking proceeding to an end and adopted four amendments governing programs that could be shown on pay cable. FCC met with broadcasters over eighteen (18) times. The FCC also met with public interest groups. After oral arguments the FCC promulgated the rule. HBO appealed, stating that there was too much *ex parte* contact.
Held: The court held that there was too much *ex parte* communication, and that the communication related to the merits of the rule. Therefore the communication should have occurred on the record, and in a hearing. The court noted that *ex parte* contact is a difficult subject because there is no official record and no opportunity for adversarial comment. Information gathered *ex parte* that becomes relevant must be disclosed at some point. If it formed a basis for agency action, it must be disclosed to the public in some form. Any *ex parte* communication between an agency official and an interested party should be placed on the record (the actual written document, or a written summary of any oral conversation).

VII.   JUDICIAL REVIEW BY HIGHER AUTHORITY

Section VII deals with requirements that parties must meet prior to seeking judicial intervention -- notably, the issues of standing and ripeness. Courts will not review a case (or agency decision) if the challenging party does not have standing. This section deals with when and who may sue in a court of law from an agency action. Furthermore, the courts will not automatically step in when a party so chooses – the case must be "ripe" for decision. Certain criteria must be met prior to the court even reviewing the case even if there is standing. This section discusses those criteria.

A.   Standing

1.   General Requirements

    a.   Injury in fact;

    b.   Causation;

    c.   Person within zone of interest to be protected by the statute.

2.   Zone of Interest

Association of Data Processing Services Organization, Inc. v. Camp, 397 U.S. 150 (1970)

Facts: The petitioner's business consisted of data processing. A new law would allow banks to compete in data processing. The question was whether a competitor of the bank would have standing to challenge the statute.

Held: The Court held that the Banking Act gave competitors the standing to sue. The Court promulgated a two part test: (1) Is there an injury in fact (economical or other)? (2) Is the injury the type of injury that the statute sought to protect against? (i.e., is the injured party within the statutory "zone of interest?") This case expanded the class of persons who may have standing and helped environmental groups achieve standing to sue on behalf of their membership.

Clarke v. SIA, 479 U.S. 388 (1987)

Facts: The Supreme Court decided to review its decision in Data Processing above. Here, banks wanted the right to broker services in and out of their state. The law only allowed for home state brokerage (the bank could not utilize its out of state branches). The Comptroller approved the banks' application, holding that out of state facilities were not "branches" within the terms of the statute. Competing brokers sued. The banks argued that brokers did not have standing because they were not in the zone of interest of the statute's protection.

Held: The Supreme Court held the brokers did have standing. The Court said competitors who would suffer economic injury have sufficient standing. The Court noted that the trend is to allow a more liberal and broader reading of standing with regard to agency action.

Air Courier v. Postal Worker's Union, 498 U.S. 517 (1991)

Facts: The Postal Service was granted a monopoly over the carrying of mail. The statute allowed suspension of monopoly anywhere the public interest so required. Pursuant to this provision, the Postal Service relaxed its monopoly in favor of private carriers for international re-mail to foreign addresses. The Postal Union sued. The private carriers alleged the Postal Union had no standing.

Held: The Supreme Court agreed that there was no standing. The Court held the statute was meant to protect the financial revenues of the federal government and the public, not the workers. The Court looked to the legislative history and intent, as well as other aspects of the legislation.

Sierra Club v. Morton, 405 U.S. 727 (1972)

Facts: A certain section of Sequoia National Park was designated as a game refuge. Therefore, the area was uncut and remained quasi-wilderness. Near the park, Disney won rights to build a ski resort with all the lifts, buildings, and roads that might accompany it. However, to service the resort, a road would have to be built through the game refuge. An environmental group sought a hearing to block the development, and sought an injunction on behalf of its membership. The District Court granted the injunction. The Court of Appeals reversed on the issue of standing.

Held: The Supreme Court held that not every group who had an interest may sue; there must be an injury. The Court held that the group had a special interest in the forest preservation (with relevant knowledge), but there was insufficient injury to allow standing.

National Credit Union Administration (NCUA) v. First National Bank & Trust Co., No. 96-843 (February 25, 1998).

Facts: The NCUA decided that section 109 of the Federal Credit Union Act, which states "federal credit union membership shall be limited to groups having a common bond of occupation or association, or to groups within a well-defined neighborhood, community, or rural district," permitted credit unions to be composed of several different unrelated groups with a single identifying characteristic. Following this decision, the NCUA approved several charter amendments allowing unrelated employer groups to form the membership of AT&T Family Federal Credit Union ("ATTF"), five commercial banks and the American Bankers Association. The ATTF brought suit alleging that the NCUA's decision was contrary to the plain wording of section 109. The District Court dismissed, finding the complaint stating that ATTF lacked standing because their interest was not in the zone of interest protected by section 109. The Court of Appeals reversed and remanded. On remand the District Court granted summary judgment against ATTF applying the test in *Chevron USA v. Natural Resources Defense Council, supra.* The Court of Appeals reversed, holding that the District Court applied the *Chevron* test incorrectly.

APA to seek court interpretation of section 109. The Supreme Court reviewed their decision under *Data Processing, supra.* The Court noted that under the "zone of interest" analysis, the relevant question is concerns the interests to be protected rather than those who are supposed to benefit from the law. The Court interpreted section 109 to limit membership in every federal credit union to members of definable groups. The Court opined that this also meant that the credit union may limit its banking services to certain members while excluding others. Members may be limited to certain distinct markets, small or large. Therefore, expansion of these markets or membership would affect the zone of interest of ATTF.

3.   Causation & Injury in Fact

Simon v. Eastern Kentucky Welfare Rights Organization., 426 U.S. 26 (1976).

Facts: Several indigents and organizations composed of indigents sued the IRS for issuing a Revenue Ruling allowing favorable tax treatment to a nonprofit hospital that offered only ER services to indigents. The petitioners alleged this was in violation of the APA and the IRS Code. The Code allowed for certain nonprofit hospitals to form corporations and receive favorable tax treatment if they qualified by operating exclusively for charitable purposes. Plaintiffs argued this would make it more difficult for indigents to receive quality medical care because the hospitals would opt to provide the minimum level of indigent services qualifying them for the tax exemption.

Held: The Supreme Court held there was no injury in fact and therefore no standing to bring suit. The Court noted that action was a private cause of action because the hospital's decision was not attributable to the federal government. The Court held that to maintain suit, both traceability and redressability are required. There must be a traceable line from the injury suffered to the agency's conduct.

Lujan v. Defenders of Wildlife, 504 U.S. 555 (1992)

Facts: The Endangered Species Act divided protection responsibilities between the Secretary of the Interior and Secretary of the Commerce. All agencies were to consult with the appropriate Secretary to make sure that any agency action would not affect endangered species. The Secretaries promulgated joint regulations on how to apply the Act in foreign nations, and then revised the Act to limit the geographic applicability to the United States and high seas. Wildlife protection groups sued saying the statute was misinterpreted. The District Court held there was no standing. This decision was reversed by the Court of Appeals. On remand, the District Court denied summary judgment on the issue of standing and granted the plaintiff's cross-motion on the merits.

Held: (Plurality decision.) The plurality held that an injury needs to be particularized. Here, the group consisted of scientists claiming that if the species disappeared they could no longer investigate and learn from them. The plurality said this injury was not particularized to the group, but was an injury suffered by all. The plurality noted that it is incumbent upon the petitioners to prove standing and injury in fact. The zone of interest arises when the group is in the realm of possible beneficiaries of the statute. The idea that they might visit a place or see the species is insufficient; actual and tangible interests must be affected.

Minority: They would have allowed a more liberal reading of standing to include such cases.

> *See also* Ohio Forestry Ass'n v. Sierra Club, -- S. Ct. - (1998); Steel Company v. Citizens for a Better Environment, 118 S. Ct. 1003 (1998); Lujan v. National Wildlife Federation, 497 U.S. 871 (1990); Gwaltney of Smithfield, Ltd. V. Chesapeake Bay Foundation, Inc., 484 U.S. 49 (1987).

B. On Review

1. Ripeness

    a. Under the rules of administrative law, a Court will only hear a case when that case has been fully dealt with by the administrative adjudication process.

    b. Exceptions

        i. Question solely of law;

        ii. Final agency action;

        iii. Hardship

            • Change in agency's conduct; or

            • Constitutional issues.

        iv. Allowed by statute

2.   **Preclusion of Judicial Review**

   a.   If a case is not ripe a court will not review it. Therefore, plaintiffs must exhaust the whole administrative process even if the outcome is a foregone conclusion.
   b.   Case is not ripe if there is no enforcement action taken.
   c.   Case is not ripe if the ALJ has not adjudicated.
   d.   The "clear and convincing" standard of proof is a reminder to the reviewing court that if there is doubt about congressional intent then the agency interpretation is valid.
   e.   Judicial review is precluded when the law mandates. APA § 701(a)(1,2).

Abbott Labs v. Gardner, 387 U.S. 136 (1967).
Facts: Congress amended the Federal Food, Drug and Cosmetic Act to require manufacturers of prescription drugs to print the "established name" of the drug "prominently and in type at least half as large as that used thereon" for any designer drugs (i.e. the use of generic name on every label). Drug manufacturers complained of the requirement and sued. The question was whether the manufacturers could sue prior to enforcement.
Held: The Supreme Court held that judicial review was possible. The Court stated there is a presumption of review unless there is clear and convincing evidence of a contrary legislative intent. The Court found that the APA has, within its whole, a presumption of judicial review. Furthermore, the Court noted that Congressional silence on the subject does not preclude judicial review. The Court held the case was ripe because the policy went into effect immediately and there was a higher cost in the new labeling and administration.

Block v. Community Nutrition Institute, 467 U.S. 340 (1984).
Facts: Congress passed a statute which authorized the Secretary of Agriculture to set the minimum price milk handlers must pay to producers for milk. The Secretary set a price for drinking milk, and another, lower price for milk in produce. Consumers and nonprofit organizations that promoted milk and nutrition in lower income families challenged the statute, arguing that reconstituted milk (milk powder sold then mixed with water) was wrongly included in the higher-priced category. The District Court dismissed the action, and the Court of Appeals reversed.

Held: The Supreme Court reversed, holding that standing was not available to any of the petitioners. The Court stated that the statute was created to apply only to producers and handlers and that those are the parties who have standing. The petitioners could overcome this presumption but did not here (§ 556(b)). Judicial review was available, but not to the petitioners. The Court feared that to allow standing in this instance would cause the agencies to shirk their administrative duties and procedures.

Bowen v. Michigan Academy, 476 U.S. 667 (1986)

Facts: The Secretary of Health and Human Services set higher reimbursement levels for "board certified" physicians than non-certified physicians for the same treatment. A medical group consisting of physicians challenged, alleging violations of the Medicare Act and the U.S. Constitution (regarding denial of a judicial forum). The lower courts agreed on statutory grounds without deciding the constitutional grounds. The Secretary appealed stating that the Act precluded judicial review.

Held: The Supreme Court held that judicial review was available. The Court noted that it is extremely rare that a statute wholly disallows judicial review and any provision which so states will be strictly construed. The Court noted that the doctors are not challenging the determination of payment but rather the computation, and held that the statute did not preclude judicial review of computation.

3. Agency Discretion

Webster v. Doe, 486 U.S. 592 (1988)

Facts: Congress passed a law which allowed the CIA Director to fire any employee when necessary or advisable in the interests of the U.S. The CIA fired an outspoken homosexual. The question was whether judicial review was allowed.

Held: The Supreme Court held that the decision was not judicially reviewable. The statute read that the Director can fire anybody when he "shall deem" it is the best interest, not "when in the best interest". This statement meant firing was at the discretion of the Director. The Court utilized APA §701(a)(2). The Court held that any constitutional question was not in the discretion of the agency. The Court remanded on the constitutional issues.

Dissent: Justice Scalia felt that the decision was solely in the discretion of the agency and not the courts.

4. Congressional Instances of Preclusion

    a.   Congress passes a law;

    b.   Congress cannot remove essential court functions;

    c.   Congressional Act must be Constitutional;

    d.   Court's review limited to due process and constitutional questions;

    e.   Court can only comment on questions of law, not fact, unless there is a due process violation;

C. Exhaustion and Finality of Administrative Remedies

1. Exhaustion

Ticor Title Insurance Co. v. FTC, 814 F.2d 731 (D.C. Cir. 1987)

Facts: Section 5(b) of the Federal Trade Commission Act authorized the FTC to initiate and prosecute claims against persons suspected of price-fixing. The FTC filed a complaint against Ticor alleging they were price-fixing. Ticor challenged section 5(b) claiming it was unconstitutional and sought injunction of any further prosecutions by the FTC.

Held: The court declined to decide the issue. The court stated that the proceedings were ongoing declined to issue a ruling on the case. The court held that petitioners must exhaust all possible administrative remedies before seeking court satisfaction. One judge held that exhaustion is required because of judicial economy and courts are not allowed to usurp the agency's powers and duties, excepting circumstances where there was a constitutional question, the possibility of irreparable harm to the parties, or a clear and unambiguous violation of law, regulation, or the Constitution. A second judge said that the case was not yet ripe. The third judge stated that courts could only intervene once the administrative proceedings were final. All administrative hearings and appeals to the agency must be over before a court is allowed to step in.

Sims v. Apfel, No. 98-9537 (June 5, 2000)

Facts: Petitioner was denied Social Security disability and Supplemental Security Income benefits. Petitioner lost a hearing before a Social Security ALJ and then was denied review by the Social Security Appeals Council. Petitioner filed an appeal with the Federal District Court alleging that the ALJ erred in three ways. The District Court denied her claim. The Fifth Circuit affirmed, concluding that they lacked jurisdiction over two of the contentions because they were not included in the request for review by the Appeals Council.

Held: The Supreme Court reversed and remanded. The Court held that a claimant who exhausts administrative remedies need not also exhaust all appeallable issues in a request for review to the Appeal Council. The Court noted that the agency's regulations did not call for exhaustion as in most cases.

Concurrence: The concurrence placed the "blame" for the lack of exhaustion of issues on the Appeals Council. The concurrence stated it was the Appeal Council who has the primary responsibility of development of issues. The concurrence noted that the agency hearings are informal and investigative, not adversarial, therefore, it was the responsibility of the ALJ and Appeal Council to develop the appealable issues.

2. Finality

Before a party may seek court intervention, the judgment of the administrative court must be final, unless otherwise statutorily authorized. If the party pursues an appeal or other recourse in the administrative setting they must exhaust such remedies.

See Abbott Labs, supra.

Digital Equipment Corp. v. Desktop Direct, Inc., 511 U.S. 863.
Held: Final decision is a decision that ends litigation on the merits and leaves nothing except execution of the judgment.

Green Tree Financial Corp.-Alabama v. Randolph, No. 99-1235 (December 11, 2000).
Facts: Respondent entered into a financing agreement with petitioners. Any contract dispute would be resolved by binding arbitration. Respondent alleged that petitioner violated the Truth in Lending Act (TILA) and that the petitioner violated the Equal Credit Opportunity Act by requiring her to arbitrate her statutory cause of action. The District Court ordered arbitration. The Eleventh Circuit reversed and held the arbitration clause unenforceable because the process did not guarantee to enforce her statutory rights because of the high arbitration costs.

Held: The Supreme Court affirmed in part and reversed in part. The Court held that where the District Court ordered the parties to arbitration and dismissed all claims before it, it was a "final decision." The Court noted however, that the contract is not unenforceable simply because it says nothing about arbitration costs. The Court noted that the Respondent bears the burden of demonstrating that the arbitration is prohibitively expensive.

D. Sovereign Immunity

Department of the Army v. Blue Fox, Inc., No. 97-1642 (January 20, 1999)

Facts: In performing work for the Army, an insolvent contractor failed to pay a subcontractor for construction work completed. The Army did not require the contractor to post any bonds to ensure payment. Blue Fox decided to sue the Army directly in federal court to assert an equitable lien on funds held by the Army. The district court held that sovereign immunity prevented Blue Fox from asserting such a claim and that the court lacked jurisdiction. The 9th Circuit reversed in part and held that *Bowen v. Massachusetts*, 487 U.S. 879 that the APA waives immunity for equitable action, thus allowing the Blue Fox claim.

Held: The Supreme Court reversed holding that Blue Fox's claim was barred by the sovereign immunity doctrine. The Court stated that § 702 did not nullify that, unless *expressly waived* by Congress, sovereign immunity bars all creditors from seeking liens against the Government.

Federal Maritime Commission v. South Carolina State Ports Authority, et al., U.S. No. 01-46 (May 28, 2002)

Facts: South Carolina Maritime Services, Inc. (Maritime Services) filed a complaint with petitioner Federal Maritime Commission (FMC), contending that respondent South Carolina State Ports Authority (SCSPA) violated the Shipping Act of 1984 when it denied Maritime Services' permission to berth a cruise ship at SCSPA's port facilities in Charleston, South Carolina. The complaint was referred to an Administrative Law Judge who found that SCSPA, an arm of the State of South Carolina, was entitled to sovereign immunity and thus dismissed the complaint. Reversing on its own motion, the FMC concluded that state sovereign immunity covered proceedings before judicial tribunals, not Executive Branch agencies. The Fourth Circuit reversed.

Held: State's sovereign immunity applied to states under dual sovereignty. Thus sovereign immunity thus barred the FMC from adjudicating a private party's complaint against a non-consenting state. Furthermore, immunity applied in Administrative proceedings because ALJs and trial judges play similar roles in adjudicative proceedings and that administrative and judicial proceedings share numerous common features. (citing *Butz v. Economou*, 438 U.S. 478 (1978)). Finally, the Court rejected the petitioner's argument that the federal government limits states' immunity by its authority to regulate maritime commerce

VIII. ADMINISTRATIVE PROCEDURE ACT

60 Stat. 237 (1946), as amended by 80 Stat. 378 (1966) as amended by 81 Stat. 54(1967), 88 Stat. 1561, 88 Stat. 1897 (1974), 89 Stat. 1057 (1975), 90 Stat. 1241, 90 Stat. 2721(1976), 5 U.S.C. §§ 551-59, 701-06, 1305, 3105, 3344, 5362, 7521.

UNITED STATES CODE, TITLE 5

Chapter 5-Administrative Procedure
Subchapter II - Administrative Procedure

§ 551. Definitions

For the purpose of this subchapter -
1) "agency" means each authority of the Government of the United States, whether or not it is within or subject to review by another agency, but does not include -

    A) the Congress;
    B) the courts of the United States;
    C) the governments of the territories or possessions of the United States;

D)   the government of the District of Columbia;
     or except as to the requirements of section 552 of this
     title -

E)   agencies composed of representatives of the parties or
     of representatives of organizations of the parties to the
     disputes determined by them;

F)   courts martial and military commissions;

G)   military authority exercised in the field in time of war
     or in occupied territory; or

H)   functions conferred by sections 1738,1739, 1743, and
     1744 of title 12; chapter 2 of title 41; or sections 1622,
     1884, 1891-1902, and former section 1641(b) (2), of
     title 50, appendix;

2)   "person" includes an individual, partnership, corporation,
     association, or public or private organization other than an
     agency;

3)   "party" includes a person or agency named or admitted as a
     party, or property seeking and entitled as of right to be
     admitted as a party, in an agency proceeding, and a person
     or agency admitted by an agency as a party for limited
     purposes;

4)   "rule" means the whole or a part of an agency statement of
     general or particular applicability and future effect designed
     to implement, interpret, or prescribe law or policy or
     describing the organization, procedure, or practice
     requirements of an agency and includes the approval or
     prescription for the future of rates, wages, corporate or
     financial structures or reorganization thereof, prices,
     facilities, appliances, services or allowances therefore or of
     valuations, costs, or accounting, or practices bearing on any
     of the foregoing;

5)   "rule making" means agency process for formulating,
     amending, or repealing a rule;

6)   "order" means the whole or a part of a final disposition,
     whether affirmative, negative, injunctive, or declaratory in
     form, of an agency in a matter other than rule making but
     including licensing;

7) "adjudication" means agency process for the formulation of an order;

8) "license" includes the whole or a part of an agency permit, certificate, approval, registration, charter, membership, statutory exemption or other form of permission;

9) "licensing" includes agency process respecting the grant, renewal, denial, revocation, suspension, annulment, withdrawal, limitation, amendment, modification, or conditioning of a license;

10) "sanction" includes the whole or a part of an agency -

A) prohibition, requirement, limitation, or other condition affecting the freedom of a person;
B) withholding of relief;
C) imposition of penalty or fine;
D) destruction, taking, seizure, or withholding of property;
E) assessment of damages, reimbursement, restitution, compensation, costs, charges, or fees;
F) requirement, revocation, or suspension of a license; or
G) taking other compulsory or restrictive action;

11) "relief" includes the whole or a part of an agency -

A) grant of money, assistance, license, authority, exemption, exception, privilege, or remedy;
B) recognition of a claim, right, immunity, privilege, exemption, or exception; or
C) taking of other action on the application or petition of, and beneficial to, a person;

12) "agency proceeding" means an agency process as defined by paragraphs (5), (7), and (9) of this section;

13) "agency action" includes the whole or a part of an agency rule, order, license, sanction, relief, or the equivalent or denial thereof, or failure to act; and

14) "*ex parte* communication" means an oral or written communication not on the public record with respect to which reasonable prior notice to all parties is not given, but it shall not include requests for status reports on any matter or proceeding covered by this subchapter.

§ 552. Public information; agency rules, opinions, orders, records, and proceedings

(a) Each agency shall make available to the public information as follows:

1) Each agency shall separately state and currently publish in the Federal Register for the guidance of the public -

A) descriptions of its central and field organization and the established places at which, the employees (and in the case of a uniformed service, the members) from whom, and the methods whereby, the public may obtain information, make submittals or requests, or obtain decisions;

B) statements of the general course and method by which its functions are channeled and determined, including the nature and requirements of all formal and informal procedures available;

C) rules of procedure, descriptions of forms available or the places at which forms may be obtained, and instructions as to the scope and contents of all papers, reports, or examinations;

D) substantive rules of general applicability adopted as authorized by law, and statements of general policy or interpretations of general applicability formulated and adopted by the agency; and

E) each amendment, revision, or repeal of the foregoing.

Except to the extent that a person has actual and timely notice of the terms thereof, a person may not in any manner be required to resort to, or be adversely affected by, a matter required to be published in the Federal Register and not so published. For the purpose of this paragraph, matter reasonably available to the class of persons affected thereby is deemed published in the Federal Register when incorporated by reference therein with the approval of the Director of the Federal Register.

2) Each agency, in accordance with published rules, shall make available for public inspection and copying -

A) final opinions, including concurring and dissenting opinions, as well as orders, made in the adjudication of cases;

B) those statements of policy and interpretations which have been adopted by the agency and are not published in the Federal Register; and

C) administrative staff manuals and instructions to staff that affect a member of the public unless the materials are promptly published and copies offered for sale. To the extent required to prevent a clearly unwarranted invasion of personal privacy, an agency may delete identifying details when it makes available or publishes an opinion, statement of policy, interpretation, or staff manual or instruction. However, in each case the justification for the deletion shall be explained fully in writing. Each agency shall also maintain and make available for public inspection and copying current indexes providing identifying information for the public as to any matter issued, adopted, or promulgated after July 4, 1967, and required by this paragraph to be made available or published. Each agency shall promptly publish, quarterly or more frequently, and distribute (by sale or otherwise) copies of each index or supplements thereto unless it determines by order published in the Federal Register that the publication would be unnecessary and impracticable, in which case the agency shall nonetheless provide copies of such index on request at a cost not to exceed the direct cost of duplication. A final order, opinion, statement of policy, interpretation, or staff manual or instruction that affects a member of the public may be relied on, used, or cited as precedent by an agency against a party other than an agency only if -

i. it has been indexed and either made available or published as provided by this paragraph; or

ii. the party has actual and timely notice of the terms thereof.

3) Except with respect to the records made available under paragraphs (1) and (2) of this subsection, each agency, upon any request for records which (A) reasonably describes such records and (B) is made in accordance with published rules stating the time, place, fees (if any), and procedures to be followed, shall make the records promptly available to any person.

A) In order to carry out the provisions of this section, each agency shall promulgate regulations, pursuant to notice and receipt of public comment, specifying a uniform schedule of fees applicable to all constituent units of such agency. Such fees shall be limited to reasonable standard charges for document search and duplication and provide for recovery of only the direct costs of such search and duplication. Documents shall be furnished without charge or at a reduced charge where the agency determines that waiver or reduction of the fee is in the public interest because furnishing the information can be considered as primarily benefiting the general public.

B) On complaint, the district court of the United States in the district in which the complainant resides, or has his principal place of business, or in which the agency records are situated, or in the District of Columbia, has jurisdiction to enjoin the agency from withholding agency records and to order the production of any agency records improperly withheld from the complainant. In such a case the court shall determine the matter de novo, and may examine the contents of such agency records in camera to determine whether such records or any part thereof shall be withheld under any of the exemptions set forth in subsection (b) of this section, and the burden is on the agency to sustain its action,

C) Notwithstanding any other provision of law, the defendant shall serve an answer or otherwise plead to any complaint made under this subsection within thirty days after service upon the defendant of the pleading in which such complaint is made, unless the court otherwise directs for good cause shown.

D) Except as to cases the court considers of greater importance, proceedings before the district court, as authorized by this subsection, and appeals there from, take precedence on the docket over all cases and shall be assigned for hearing and trial or for argument at the earliest practicable date and expedited in every way.

E) The court may assess against the United States reasonable attorney fees and other litigation costs reasonably incurred in any case under this section in which the complainant has substantially prevailed.

F) Whenever the court orders the production of any agency records improperly withheld from the complainant and assesses against the United States reasonable attorney fees and other litigation costs, and the court additionally issues a written finding that the circumstances surrounding the withholding raise questions whether agency personnel acting arbitrarily or capriciously with respect to the withholding, the Civil Service Commission shall promptly initiate a proceeding to determine whether disciplinary action is warranted against the officer or employee who was primarily responsible for the withholding. The Commission, after investigation and consideration of the evidence submitted, shall submit its findings and recommendations to the administrative authority of the agency concerned and shall send copies of the findings and recommendations to the officer or employee or his representative. The administrative authority shall take the corrective action that the Commission recommends.

G) In the event of noncompliance with the order of the court, the district court may punish for contempt the responsible employee, and in the case of a uniformed service, the responsible member.

4) Intentionally blank

5) Each agency having more than one member shall maintain and make available for public inspection a record of the final votes of each member in every agency proceeding.

6)   A) Each agency, upon any request for records made under paragraph (1), (2), or (3) of this subsection, shall -

      i.   determine within ten days (excepting Saturdays, Sundays, and legal public holidays) after the receipt of any such request whether to comply with such request and shall immediately notify the person making such request of such determination and the reasons therefore, and of the right of such person to appeal to the head of the agency any adverse determination; and

      ii. make a determination with respect to any appeal within twenty days (excepting Saturdays, Sundays, and legal public holidays) after the receipt of such appeal. If on appeal the denial of the request for records is in whole or in part upheld, the agency shall notify the person making such request of the provisions for judicial review of that determination under paragraph (4) of this subsection.

    B) In unusual circumstances as specified in this subparagraph, the time limits prescribed in either clause (i) or clause (ii) of subparagraph (A) may be extended by written notice to the person making such request setting forth the reasons for such extension and the date on which a determination is expected to be dispatched. No such notice shall specify a date that would result in an extension for more than ten working days. As used in this subparagraph, "unusual circumstances means, but only to the extent reasonably necessary to the proper processing of the particular request -

      i.   the need to search for and collect the requested records from field facilities or other establishments that are separate from the office processing the request;

      ii. the need to search for, collect, and appropriately examine a voluminous amount of separate and distinct records which are demanded in a single request; or

      iii. the need for consultation, which shall be conducted with all practicable speed, with another agency having a substantial interest in the determination of the request or among two or more components of the agency having substantial subject-matter interest therein.

C) Any person making a request to any agency for records under paragraph (1), (2), or (3) of this subsection shall be deemed to have exhausted his administrative remedies with respect to such request if the agency fails to comply with the applicable time limit provisions of this paragraph. If the Government can show exceptional circumstances exist and that the agency is exercising due diligence in responding to the request, the court may retain jurisdiction and allow the agency additional time to complete its review of the records. Upon any determination by an agency to comply with a request for records, the records shall be made promptly available to such person making such request. Any notification of denial of any request for records under this subsection shall set forth the names and titles or positions of each person responsible for the denial of such request.

b) This section does not apply to matters that are -

1) (A) specifically authorized under criteria established by an Executive order to be kept secret in the interest of national defense or foreign policy and (B) are in fact properly classified pursuant to such Executive order;

2) related solely to the internal personnel rules and practices of an agency;

3) specifically exempted from disclosure by statute (other than section 552b of this title), provided that such statute (A) requires that the matters be withheld from the public in such a manner as to leave no discretion on the issue, or (B) establishes particular criteria for withholding or refers to particular types of matters to be withheld;

4) trade secrets and commercial or financial information obtained from a person and privileged or confidential;

5) inter-agency or intra-agency memorandums or letters which would not be available by law to a party other than an agency in litigation with the agency;

6) personnel and medical files and similar files the disclosure of which would constitute a clearly unwarranted invasion of personal privacy;

7) investigatory records compiled for law enforcement purposes, but only to the extent that the production of such records would (A) interfere with enforcement proceedings, (B) deprive a person of a right to a fair trial or an impartial adjudication, (C) constitute an unwarranted invasion of personal privacy, (D) disclose the identity of a confidential source and, in the case of a record compiled by a criminal law enforcement authority in the course of a criminal investigation, or by an agency conducting a lawful national security intelligence investigation, confidential information furnished only by the confidential source, (E) disclose investigative techniques and procedures, or (F) endanger the life or physical safety of law enforcement personnel;

8) contained in or related to examination, operating, or condition reports prepared by, on behalf of, or for the use of an agency responsible for the regulation or supervision of financial institutions; or

9) geological and geophysical information and data, including maps, concerning wells. Any reasonably segregable portion of a record shall be provided to any person requesting such record after deletion of the portions which are exempt under this subsection.

c) This section does not authorize withholding of information or limit the availability of records to the public, except as specifically stated in this section. This section is not authority to withhold information from Congress.

d) On or before March 1 of each calendar year, each agency shall submit a report covering the preceding calendar year to the Speaker of the House of Representatives and President of the Senate for referral to the appropriate committees of the Congress. The report shall include -

1) the number of determinations made by such agency not to comply with requests for records made to such agency under subsection (a) and the reasons for each such determination;

2) the number of appeals made by persons under subsection (a)(6), the result of such appeals, and the reason for the action upon each appeal that results in a denial of information;

3) the names and titles or positions of each person responsible for the denial of records requested under this section, and the number of instances of participation for each;

4) the results of each proceeding conducted pursuant to subsection (a) (4) (F), including a report of the disciplinary action taken against the officer or employee who was primarily responsible for improperly withholding records or an explanation of why disciplinary action was not taken;

5) a copy of every rule made by such agency regarding this section;

6) a copy of the fee schedule and the total amount of fees collected by the agency for making records available under this section; and

7) other information that indicates efforts to administer fully this section.

The Attorney General shall submit an annual report on or before March 1 of each calendar year which shall include for the prior calendar year a listing of the number of cases arising under this section, the exemption involved in each case, the disposition of such case, and the cost, fees, and penalties assessed under subsections (a) (4) (E), (F), and (G). Such report shall also include a description of the efforts undertaken by the Department of Justice to encourage agency compliance with this section.

e) For purposes of this section, the term "agency" as defined in section 551(1) of this title includes any executive department, military department, Government corporation, Government controlled corporation, or other establishment in the executive branch of the Government (including the Executive Office of the President), or any independent regulatory agency.

§ 552a. Records maintained on individuals

a) **Definitions.** - For purposes of this section -

1) the term "agency" means agency as defined in section 552(e) of this title;

2) the term "individual" means a citizen of the United States or an alien lawfully admitted for permanent residence;

3) the term "maintain" includes maintain, collect, use, or disseminate;

4) the term "record" means any item, collection, or grouping of information about an individual that is maintained by an agency, including, but not limited to, his education, financial transactions, medical history, and criminal or employment history and that contains his name, or the identifying number, symbol, or other identifying particular assigned to the individual, such as a finger or voice print or a photograph;

5) the term "system of records" means a group of any records under the control of any agency from which information is retrieved by the name of the individual or by some identifying number, symbol, or other identifying particular assigned to the individual;

6) the term "statistical record" means a record in a system of records maintained for statistical research or reporting purposes only and not used in whole or in part in making any determination about an identifiable individual, except as provided by section 8 of title 13; and

7) the term "routine use" means, with respect to the disclosure of a record, the use of such record for a purpose which is compatible with the purpose for which it was collected.

b) **Conditions of disclosure.** - No agency shall disclose any record which is contained in a system of records by any means of communication to any person, or to another agency, except pursuant to a written request by, or with the prior written consent of, the individual to whom the record pertains, unless disclosure of the record would be -

1) to those officers and employees of the agency which maintains the record who have a need for the record in the performance of their duties;

2) required under section 552 of this title;

3) for a routine use as defined in subsection (a)(7) of this

section and described under subsection (e)(4)(D) of this section;

4) to the Bureau of the Census for purposes of planning or carrying out a census or survey or related activity pursuant to the provisions of title 13;

5) to a recipient who has provided the agency with advance adequate written assurance that the record will be used solely as a statistical research or reporting record, and the record is to be transferred in a form that is not individually identifiable;

6) to the National Archives of the United States as a record which has sufficient historical or other value to warrant its continued preservation by the United States Government, or for evaluation by the Administrator of General Services or his designee to determine whether the record has such value;

7) to another agency or to an instrumentality of any governmental jurisdiction within or under the control of the United States for a civil or criminal law enforcement activity if the activity is authorized by law, and if the head of the agency or instrumentality has made a written request to the agency which maintains the record specifying the particular portion desired and the law enforcement activity for which the record is sought;

8) to a person pursuant to a showing of compelling circumstances affecting the health or safety of an individual if upon such disclosure notification is transmitted to the last known address of such individual;

9) to either House of Congress, or, to the extent of matter within its jurisdiction, any committee or subcommittee thereof, any joint committee of Congress or subcommittee of any such joint committee;

10) to the Comptroller General, or any of his authorized representatives, in the course of the performance of the duties of the General Accounting Office; or

11) pursuant to the order of a court of competent jurisdiction.

c) **Accounting of Certain Disclosures**. - Each agency, with respect to each system of records under its control, shall -

1) except for disclosures made under subsections (b)(1) or (b)(2) of this section, keep an accurate accounting of -
   A) the date, nature, and purpose of each disclosure of a record to any person or to another agency made under

subsection (b) of this section; and is

B) the name and address of the person or agency to whom the disclosure made;

2) retain the accounting made under paragraph (1) of this subsection for at least five years or the life of the record, whichever is longer, after the disclosure for which the accounting is made;

3) except for disclosures made under subsection (b)(7) of this section, make the accounting made under paragraph (1) of this subsection available to the individual named in the record at his request; and

4) inform any person or other agency about any correction or notation of dispute made by the agency in accordance with subsection (d) of this section of any record that has been disclosed to the person or agency if an accounting of the disclosure was made.

d) **Access to records.** - Each agency that maintains a system of records shall -

1) upon request by an individual to gain access to his record or to any information pertaining to him which is contained in the system, permit him and upon his request, a person of his own choosing to accompany him, to review the record and have a copy made of all or any portion thereof in a form comprehensible to him, except that the agency may require the individual *to* furnish a written statement authorizing discussion of that individual's record in the accompanying person's presence;

2) permit the individual to request amendment of a record pertaining to him and -
   A) not later than 10 days (excluding Saturdays, Sundays, and legal public holidays) after the date of receipt of such request, acknowledge in writing such receipt; and
   B) promptly, either -
      i. make any correction of any portion thereof which the individual believes is not accurate, relevant, timely, or complete; or
      ii. inform the individual of its refusal to amend the record in accordance with his request, the reason for the refusal, the procedures established by the agency for the individual to request a review of that

refusal by the head of the agency or an officer designated by the head of the agency, and the name and business address of that official;

3) permit the individual who disagrees with the refusal of the agency to amend his record to request a review of such refusal, and not later than 3~ days (excluding Saturdays, Sundays, and legal public holidays) from the date on which the individual requests such review, complete such review and make a final determination unless, for good cause shown, the head of the agency extends such 30-day period; and if, after his review, the reviewing official also refuses to amend the record in accordance with the request, permit the individual to file with the agency a concise statement setting forth the reasons for his disagreement with the refusal of the agency, and notify the individual of the provisions for judicial review of the reviewing official's determination under subsection (g)(l)(A) of this section;

4) in any disclosure, containing information about which the individual has filed a statement of disagreement, occurring after the filing of the statement under paragraph (3) of this subsection, clearly note any portion of the record which is disputed and provide copies of the statement and, if the agency deems it appropriate, copies of a concise statement of the reasons of the agency for not making the amendments requested, to persons or other agencies to whom the disputed record has been disclosed; and

5) nothing in this section shall allow an individual access to any information compiled in reasonable anticipation of a civil action or proceeding.

e) **Agency requirements**. - Each agency that maintains a system of records shall -

1) maintain in its records only such information about an individual as is relevant and necessary to accomplish a purpose of the agency required to be accomplished by statute or by executive order of the President;

2) collect information to the greatest extent practicable directly from the subject individual when the information may result in adverse determinations about an individual's rights, benefits, and privileges under Federal programs;

3) inform each individual whom it asks to supply information,

on the form which it uses to collect the information or on a separate form that can be retained by the individual -

A) the authority (whether granted by statute, or by executive order of the President) which authorizes the solicitation of the information and whether disclosure of such information is mandatory or voluntary;

B) the principal purpose or purposes for which the information is intended to be used;

C) the routine uses which may be made of the information, as published pursuant to paragraph (4)(D) of this subsection; and

D) the effects on him, if any, of not providing all or any part of the requested information;

4) subject to the provisions of paragraph (11) of this subsection, publish in the Federal Register at least annually a notice of the existence and character of the system of records, which notice shall include -

A) the name and location of the system;

B) the categories of individuals on whom records are maintained in the system;

C) the categories of records maintained in the system;

D) each routine use of the records contained in the system, including the categories of users and the purpose of such use;

E) the policies and practices of the agency regarding storage, retrievability, access controls, retention, and disposal of the records;

F) the title and business address of the agency official who is responsible for the system of records;

G) the agency procedures whereby an individual can be notified at his request if the system of records contains a record pertaining to him;

H) the agency procedures whereby an individual can be notified at his request how he can gain access to any record pertaining to him contained in the system of records, and how he can contest its content; and

I) the categories of sources of records in the system;

5) Maintain all records which are used by the agency in making any determination about any individual with such accuracy, relevance, timeliness, and completeness as is

reasonably necessary to assure fairness to the individual in the determination;

6) prior to disseminating any record about an individual to any person other than an agency, unless the dissemination is made pursuant to subsection (b) (2) of this section, make reasonable efforts to assure that such records are accurate, complete, timely, and relevant for agency purposes;

7) maintain no record describing how any individual exercises rights guaranteed by the First Amendment unless expressly authorized by statute or by the individual about whom the record is maintained or unless pertinent to and within the scope of an authorized law enforcement activity;

8) make reasonable efforts to serve notice on an individual when any record on such individual is made available to any person under compulsory legal process when such process becomes a matter of public record;

9) establish rules of conduct for persons involved in the design, development, operation, or maintenance of any system of records, or in maintaining any record, and instruct each such person with respect to such rules and the requirements of this section, including any other rules and procedures adopted pursuant to this section and the penalties for noncompliance;

10) establish appropriate administrative, technical, and physical safeguards to insure the security and confidentiality of records and to protect against any anticipated threats or hazards to their security or integrity which could result in substantial harm, embarrassment, inconvenience, or unfairness to any individual on whom information is maintained; and

11) at least 30 days prior to publication of information under paragraph (4) (D) of this subsection, publish in the Federal Register notice of any new use or intended use of the information in the system, and provide an opportunity for interested persons to submit written data, views, or arguments to the agency.

f) **Agency rules**. - In order to carry out the provisions of this section, each agency that maintains a system of records shall promulgate rules, in accordance with the requirements (including general notice) of section 553 of this title, which shall:

1) establish procedures whereby an individual can be notified in response to his request if any system of records named by the individual contains a record pertaining to him;

2) define reasonable times, places, and requirements for identifying an individual who requests his record or information pertaining to him before the agency shall make the record or information available to the individual;

3) establish procedures for the disclosure to an individual upon his request of his record or information pertaining to him, including special procedure, if deemed necessary, for the disclosure to an individual of medical records, including psychological records, pertaining to him;

4) establish procedures for reviewing a request from an individual concerning the amendment of any record or information pertaining to the individual, for making a determination on the request, for an appeal within the agency of an initial adverse agency determination, and for whatever additional means may be necessary for each individual to be able to exercise fully his rights under this section; and

5) establish fees to be charged, if any, to any individual for making copies of his record, excluding the cost of any search' for and review of the record.

The Office of the Federal Register shall annually compile and publish the rules promulgated under this subsection and agency notices published under subsection (e)(4) of this section in a form available to the public at low cost.

g) **(l) Civil remedies**. - Whenever any agency

A) makes a determination under subsection (d)(3) of this section not to amend an individual's record in accordance with his request, or fails to make such review in conformity with that subsection;

B) refuses to comply with an individual request under subsection (d)(1) of this section;

C) fails to maintain any record concerning any individual with such accuracy, relevance, timeliness, and completeness as is necessary to assure fairness in any determination relating to the qualifications, character, rights, or opportunities of, or benefits to the individual that may be made on the basis of such record, and consequently a determination is made which is adverse to the individual; or

D) fails to comply with any other provision of this section, or any rule promulgated there under, in such a way as to have an adverse effect on an individual, the individual may bring a civil action against the agency, and the district courts of the United States shall have jurisdiction in the matters under the provisions of this subsection.

2) A) In any suit brought under the provisions of subsection (g)(1)(A) of this section, the court may order the agency to amend the individual's record in accordance with his request or in such other way as the court may direct. In such a case the court shall determine the matter de novo.

B) The court may assess against the United States reasonable attorney fees and other litigation costs reasonably incurred in any case under this paragraph in which the complainant has substantially prevailed.

3) A) In any suit brought under the provisions of subsection (g)(1)(B) of this section, the court may enjoin the agency from withholding the records and order the production to the complainant of any agency records improperly withheld from him. In such a case the court shall determine the matter de novo, and may examine the contents of any agency records in camera to determine whether the records or any portion thereof may be withheld under any of the exemptions set forth in subsection (k) of this section, and the burden is on the agency to sustain its action.

B) The court may assess against the United States reasonable attorney fees and other litigation costs reasonably incurred in any case under this paragraph in which the complainant has substantially prevailed.

4) In any suit brought under the provisions of subsection (g)(1)(C) or (D) of this section in which the court determines that the agency acted in a manner which was intentional or willful, the United States shall be liable to the individual in an amount equal to the sum of -

A) actual damages sustained by the individual as a result of the refusal or failure, but in no case shall a person entitled to recovery receive less than the sum of $1,000; and

B) the costs of the action together with reasonable attorney fees as determined by the court.

5) An action to enforce any liability created under this section may be brought in the district court of the United States in the district in which the complainant resides, or has his principal place of business, or in which the agency records are situated, or in the District of Columbia, without regard to the amount in controversy, within two years from the date on which the cause of action arises, except that where an agency has materially and willfully misrepresented any information required under this section to be disclosed to an individual and the information so misrepresented is material to establishment of the liability of the agency to the individual under this section, the action may be brought at any time within two years after discovery by the individual of the misrepresentation. Nothing in this section shall be construed to authorize any civil action by reason of any injury sustained as the result of a disclosure of a record prior to September 27, 1975.

h) **Rights of legal guardians**. - For the purposes of this section, the parent of any minor, or the legal guardian of any individual who has been declared to be incompetent due to physical or mental incapacity or age by a court of competent jurisdiction, may act on behalf of the individual.

i) 1) **Criminal penalties.** - Any officer or employee of an agency, who by virtue of his employment or official position, has possession of, or access to, agency records which contain individually identifiable information the disclosure of which is prohibited by this section or by rules or regulations established there under, and who knowing that disclosure of the specific material is so prohibited, willfully discloses the material in any manner to any person or agency not entitled to receive it, shall be guilty of a misdemeanor and fined not more than $5,000.

2) Any officer or employee of any agency who willfully maintains a system of records without meeting the notice requirements of subsection (e)(4) of this section shall be guilty of a misdemeanor and fined not more than $5,000.

3) Any person who knowingly and willfully requests or obtains any record concerning an individual from an

agency under false pretenses shall be guilty of a misdemeanor and fined not more than $5,000.

j) General exemptions. - The head of any agency may promulgate rules, in accordance with the requirements (including general notice) of sections 553(b)(l), (2), and (3), (c), and (e) of this title, to exempt any system of records within the agency from any part of this section except subsections (b), (c)(l) and (2), (e)(4)(A) through (F), (e)(6), (7), (9), (10), and (11), and (i) if the system of records is -

1) maintained by the Central Intelligence Agency; or
2) maintained by an agency or component thereof which performs as its principal function any activity pertaining to the enforcement of criminal laws, including police efforts to prevent, control, or reduce crime or to apprehend criminals, and the activities of prosecutors, courts, correctional, probation, pardon, or parole authorities, and which consists of (A) information compiled for the purpose of identifying individual criminal offenders and alleged offenders and consisting only of identifying data and notations of arrests, the nature and disposition of criminal charges, sentencing, confinement, release, and parole and probation status; (B) information compiled for the purpose of a criminal investigation, including reports of informants and investigators, and associated with an identifiable individual; or (C) reports identifiable to an individual compiled at any stage of the process of enforcement of the criminal laws from arrest or indictment through release from supervision.

At the time rules are adopted under this subsection, the agency shall include in the statement required under section 553(c) of this title, the reasons why the system of records is to be exempted from a provision of this section.

k) Specific exemptions. - The head of any agency may promulgate rules, in accordance with the requirements (including general notice) of sections 553(b)(1), (2), and (3), (c), and (e) of this title, to exempt any system of records within the agency from subsections (c)(3), (d), (e)(1), (e)(4)(G), (H), and (I) and (f) of this section if the system of records is -

1) subject to the provisions of section 552 (b)(1) of this title;
2) investigatory material compiled for law enforcement

purposes, other than material within the scope of subsection (j)(2) of this section: *Provided, however,* that if any individual is denied any right, privilege, or benefit that he would otherwise be entitled by Federal law, or for which he would otherwise be eligible, as a result of the maintenance of such material, such material shall be provided to such individual, except to the extent that the disclosure of such material would reveal the identity of a source who furnished information to the Government under an express promise that the identity of the source would be held in confidence, or prior to the effective date of this section, under an implied promise that the identity of the source would be held in confidence;

3) maintained in connection with providing protective services to the President of the United States or other individuals pursuant to section 3056 of title 18;

4) required by statute to be maintained and used solely as statistical records;

5) investigatory material compiled solely for the purpose of determining suitability, eligibility, or qualifications for Federal civilian employment, military service, Federal contracts, or access to classified information, but only to the extent that the disclosure of such material would reveal the identity of a source who furnished information to the Government under an express promise that the identity of the source would be held in confidence, or, prior to the effective date of this section, under an implied promise that the identity of the source would be held in confidence;

6) testing or examination material used solely to determine individual qualifications for appointment or promotion in the Federal service the disclosure of which would compromise the objectivity or fairness of the testing or examination process; or

7) evaluation material used to determine potential for promotion in the armed services, but only to the extent that the disclosure of such material would reveal the identity of a source who furnished information to the Government under an express promise that the identity of the source would be held in confidence, or, prior to the effective date of this section, under an implied promise that the identity of the source would be held in confidence.

At the time rules are adopted under this subsection, the agency shall include in the statement required under section 553(c) of this title, the reasons why the system of records is to be exempted from a provision of this section.

l) 1) Archival Records. - Each agency record which is accepted by the Administrator of General Services for storage, processing, and servicing in accordance with section 3103 of title 44 shall, for the purposes of this section, be considered to be maintained by the agency which deposited the record and shall be subject to the provisions of this section. The Administrator of General Services shall not disclose the record except to the agency which maintains the record, or under rules established by that agency which are not inconsistent with the provisions of this section.

    2) Each agency record pertaining to an identifiable individual which was transferred to the National Archives of the United States as a record which has sufficient historical or other value to warrant its continued preservation by the United States Government, prior to the effective date of this section, shall, for the purposes of this section, be considered to be maintained by the National Archives and shall not *be* subject to the provisions of this section, except that a statement generally describing such records (modeled after the requirements relating to records subject to subsections (e) (4) (A) through (G) of this section) shall be published in the Federal Register.

    3) Each agency record pertaining to an identifiable individual which is transferred to the National Archives of the United States is a record which has sufficient historical or other value to warrant its continued preservation by the United States Government, on or after the effective date of this section, shall, for the purposes of this section, be considered to be maintained by the National Archives and shall be exempt from the requirements of this section except subsections (e) (4) (A) through (G) and (e) (9) of this section.

m) Government contractors. - When an agency provides by a contract for the operation by or on behalf of the agency of a system of records to accomplish an agency function, the agency shall, consistent with its authority, cause the requirements of this section to be applied to such system. For purposes of subsection (i) of this section any such contractor and any employee of such contractor, if such contract is agreed to on or after the effective date of this section, shall be considered to be an employee of an agency.

n) **Mailing lists**. - An individual's name and address may not be sold or rented by an agency unless such action is specifically authorized by law. This provision shall not be construed to require the withholding of names and addresses otherwise permitted to be made public.

o) **Report on new system**. - Each agency shall provide adequate advance notice to Congress and the Office of Management and Budget of any proposal to establish or alter any system of records in order to permit an evaluation of the probable or potential effect of such proposal on the privacy and other personal or property rights of individuals or the disclosure of information relating to such individuals, and its effect on the preservation of- the constitutional principles of federalism and separation of powers.

p) **Annual report**. - The President shall submit to the Speaker of the House and the President of the Senate, by June 30 of each calendar year, a consolidated report, separately listing for each Federal agency the number of records contained in any system of records which were exempted from the application of this section under the provisions of subsections (j) and (k) of this section during the preceding calendar year, and the reasons for the exemptions, and such other information as indicates efforts to administer fully this section.

q) **Effect of other laws**. - No agency shall rely on any exemption contained in section 552 of this title to withhold from an individual any record which is otherwise accessible to such individual under the provisions of this section.

§ 552b. Open meetings

a) For purposes of this section -

    1) the term "agency" means any agency, as defined in section 551 of this title, headed by a collegial body composed of two or more individual members, a majority of whom are

> appointed to such position by the President with the advice and consent of the Senate, and any subdivision thereof authorized to act on behalf of the agency;
>
> 2)   the term "meeting" means the deliberations of at least the number of individual agency members required to take action on behalf of the agency where such deliberations determine or result in the joint conduct or disposition of official agency business, but does not include deliberations required or permitted by subsection (d) or (e); and
>
> 3)   the term "member" means an individual who belongs to a collegial body heading an agency.

b)   Members shall not jointly conduct or dispose of agency business other than in accordance with this section. Except as provided in subsection (c), every portion of every meeting of an agency shall be open to public observation.

c)   Except in a case where the agency finds that the public interest requires otherwise, the second sentence of subsection (b) shall not apply to any portion of an agency meeting, and the requirements of subsections (d) and (e) shall not apply to any information pertaining to such meeting otherwise required by this section to be disclosed to the public, where the agency properly determines that such portion or portions of its meeting or the disclosure of such information is likely to -

> 1)   disclose matters that are (A) specifically authorized under criteria established by an Executive order to be kept secret in the interests of national defense or foreign policy and (B) in fact properly classified pursuant to such Executive order;
>
> 2)   relate solely to the internal personnel rules and practices of an agency;
>
> 3)   disclose matters specifically exempted from disclosure by statute (other than section 552 of this title), provided that such statute (A) requires that the matters be withheld from the public in such a manner as to leave no discretion on the issue, or (B) establishes particular criteria for withholding or refers to particular types of matters to be withheld;
>
> 4)   disclose trade secrets and commercial or financial information obtained from a person and privileged or confidential;
>
> 5)   involve accusing any person of a crime, or formally censuring any person;
>
> 6)   disclose information of a personal nature where disclosure

would constitute a clearly unwarranted invasion of personal privacy;

7) disclose investigatory records compiled for law enforcement purposes, or information which if written would be contained in such records, but only to the extent that the production of such records or information would (A) interfere with enforcement proceedings, (B) deprive a person of a right to a fair trial or an impartial adjudication, (C) constitute an unwarranted invasion of personal privacy, (D) disclose the identity of a confidential source and, in the case of a record compiled by a criminal law enforcement authority in the course of a criminal investigation, or by an agency conducting a lawful national security intelligence investigation, confidential information furnished only by the confidential source, (E) disclose investigative techniques and procedures, or (F) endanger the life or physical safety of law enforcement personnel;

8) disclose information contained in or related to examination, operating, or condition reports prepared by, on behalf of, or for the use of an agency responsible for the regulation or supervision of financial institutions;

9) disclose information the premature disclosure of which would -

A) in the case of an agency which regulates currencies, securities, commodities, or financial institutions, be likely to (i) lead to significant financial speculation in currencies, securities, or commodities, or (ii) significantly endanger the stability of any financial institution; or

B) in the case of any agency, be likely to significantly frustrate implementation of a proposed agency action, except that subparagraph (B) shall not apply in any instance where the agency has already disclosed to the public the content or nature of its proposed action, or where the agency is required by law to make such disclosure on its own initiative prior to taking final agency action on such proposal; or

10) specifically concern the agency's issuance of a subpoena, or the agency's participation in a civil action or proceeding. an action in a foreign court or international tribunal or an arbitration, or the initiation, conduct, or disposition by the

agency of a particular case of formal agency adjudication pursuant to the procedures in section 554 of this title or otherwise involving a determination on the record after opportunity for a hearing.

d) 1) Action under subsection (c) shall be taken only when a majority of the entire membership of the agency (as defined in subsection (a)(1)) votes to take such action. A separate vote of the agency members shall be taken with respect to each agency meeting a portion or portions of which are proposed to be closed to the public pursuant to subsection (c), or with respect to any information which is proposed to be withheld under subsection (c). A single vote may be taken with respect to a series of meetings, a portion or portions of which are proposed to be closed to the public, or with respect to any information concerning such series of meetings, so long as each meeting in such series involves the same particular matters and is scheduled to be held no more than thirty days after the initial meeting in such series. The vote of each agency member participating in such vote shall be recorded and no proxies shall be allowed.

2) Whenever any person whose interests may be directly affected by a portion of a meeting requests that the agency close such portion to the public for any of the reasons referred to in paragraph (5), (6), or (7) of subsection (c), the agency, upon request of any one of its members, shall vote by recorded vote whether to close such meeting.

3) Within one day of any vote taken pursuant to paragraph (1) or (2), the agency shall make publicly available a written copy of such vote reflecting the vote of each member on the question. If a portion of a meeting is to be closed to the public, the agency shall, within one day of the vote taken pursuant to paragraph (1) or (2) of this subsection, make publicly available a full written explanation of its action closing the portion together with a list of all persons expected to attend the meeting and their affiliation.

4) Any agency, a majority of whose meetings may properly be closed to the public pursuant to paragraph (4), (8), (9)(A), or (10) of subsection (c), or any combination thereof, may provide by regulation for the closing of such meetings or portions thereof in the event that a majority of the members of the agency votes by recorded vote at the beginning of

such meeting, a portion thereof, to close the exempt portion or portions of the meeting, and a copy of such vote, reflecting the vote of each member on the question, is made available to the public. The provisions of paragraphs (1), (2), and (3) of this subsection and subsection (e) shall not apply to any portion of a meeting to which such regulations apply: *Provided,* That the agency shall, except to the extent that such information is exempt from disclosure under the provisions of subsection (c), provide the public with public announcement of the time, place, and subject matter of the meeting and of each portion thereof at the earliest practicable time.

e) 1) In the case of each meeting, the agency shall make public announcement, at least one week before the meeting, of the time, place, and subject matter of the meeting, whether it is to be open or closed to the public, and the name and phone number of the official designated by the agency to respond to requests for information about the meeting. Such announcement shall be made unless a majority of the members of the agency determines by a recorded vote that agency business requires that such meeting be called at an earlier date, in which case the agency shall make public announcement of the time, place, and subject matter of such meeting, and whether open or closed to the public, at the earliest practicable time.

2) The time or place of a meeting may *be* changed following the public announcement required by paragraph (1) only if the agency publicly announces such change at the earliest practicable time. The subject matter of a meeting, or the determination of the agency to open or close a meeting, or portion of a meeting, to the public, may be changed following the public announcement required by this subsection only if (A) a majority of the entire membership of the agency determines by a recorded vote that agency business so requires and that no earlier announcement of the change was possible, and (B) the agency publicly announces such change and the vote of each member upon such change at the earliest practicable time.

3) Immediately following each public announcement required by this subsection, notice of the time, place, and subject

matter of a meeting, whether the meeting is open or closed, any change in one of the preceding, and the name and phone number of the official designated by the agency to respond to requests for information about the meeting, shall also be submitted for publication in the Federal Register.

f) 1) For every meeting closed pursuant to paragraphs (1) through (10) of subsection (c), the General Counsel or chief legal officer of the agency shall publicly certify that, in his or her opinion, the meeting may be closed to the public and shall state each relevant exemptive provision. A copy of such certification, together with a statement from the presiding officer of the meeting setting forth the time and place of the meeting, and the persons present, shall be retained by the agency. The agency shall maintain a complete transcript or electronic recording adequate to record fully the proceedings of each meeting, or portion of a meeting, closed to the public, except that in the case of a meeting, or portion of a meeting, closed to the public pursuant to paragraph (8), (9)(A), or (10) of subsection (c), the agency shall maintain either such a transcript or recording, or a set of minutes. Such minutes shall fully and clearly describe all matters discussed and shall provide a full and accurate summary of any actions taken, and the reasons therefore, including a description of each of the views expressed on any item and the record of any roll-call vote (reflecting the vote of each member on the question). All documents considered in connection with any action shall be identified in such minutes.

2) The agency shall make promptly available to the public, in a place easily accessible to the public, the transcript, electronic recording, or minutes (as required by paragraph (1)) of the discussion of any item on the agenda, or of any item of the testimony of any witness received at the meeting, except for such item or items of such discussion or testimony as the agency determines to contain information which may be withheld under subsection (c), Copies of such transcript, or minutes, or a transcription of such recording disclosing the identity of each speaker, shall be furnished to any person at the actual cost of duplication or transcription. The agency shall maintain a complete verbatim copy of the transcript, a complete copy of the minutes, or a complete

electronic recording of each meeting, or portion of a meeting, closed to the public, for a period of at least two years after such meeting, or until one year after the conclusion of any agency proceeding with respect to which the meeting or portion was held, whichever occurs later.

g) Each agency subject to the requirements of this section shall, within 180 days after the date of enactment of this section, following consultation with the Office of the Chairman of the Administrative Conference of the United States and published notice in the Federal Register of at least thirty days and opportunity for written comment by any person, promulgate regulations to implement the requirements of subsections (b) through (f) of this section. Any person may bring a proceeding in the United States District Court for the District of Columbia to require an agency to promulgate such regulations if such agency has not promulgated such regulations within the time period specified herein. Subject to any limitations of time provided by law, any person may bring a proceeding in the United States Court of Appeals for the District of Columbia to set aside agency regulations issued pursuant to this subsection that are not in accord with the requirements of subsections (b) through (f) of this section and to require the promulgation of regulations that are in accord with such subsections.

h) 1) The district courts of the United States shall have jurisdiction to enforce the requirements of subsections (b) through (f) of this section by declaratory judgment, injunctive relief, or other relief as may be appropriate. Such actions may be brought by any person against an agency prior to, or within sixty days after, the meeting out of which the violation of this section arises, except that if public announcement of such meeting is not initially provided by the agency in accordance with the requirements of this section, such action may be instituted pursuant to this section at any time prior to sixty days after any public announcement of such meeting. Such actions may be brought in the district court of the United States for the district in which the agency meeting is held or in which the agency in question has its headquarters, or in the District Court for the District of Columbia. In such actions a defendant shall serve his answer within thirty days after the service of the complaint. The burden is on the defendant to sustain his action. In deciding such cases the court may examine in camera any portion of the transcript, electronic recording, or minutes of a meeting closed to the public, and may take such additional evidence as it deems necessary. The court, having due regard for orderly administration and the public interest, as well as the interests of the parties, may grant such equitable relief as it deems appropriate, including granting an injunction against future violations of this section or ordering the agency to make available to the public such portion of the transcript, recording, or minutes of a meeting as is not authorized to be withheld under subsection (c) of this section.

2) Any Federal court otherwise authorized by law to review agency action may, at the application of any person properly participating in the proceeding pursuant to other applicable law, inquire into violations by the agency of the requirements of this section and afford such relief as it deems appropriate. Nothing in this section authorizes any Federal court having jurisdiction solely on the basis of paragraph (1) to set aside, enjoin, or invalidate any agency action (other than an action to close a meeting or to withhold information under this section) taken or discussed at any agency meeting out of which the violation of this section arose.

i) The court may assess against any party reasonable attorney fees and other litigation costs reasonably incurred by any other party who substantially prevails in any action brought in accordance with the provisions of subsection (g) or (h) of this section, except that costs may be assessed against the plaintiff only where the court finds that the suit was initiated by the plaintiff primarily for frivolous or dilatory purposes. In the case of assessment of costs against an agency, the costs may be assessed by the court against the United States.

j) Each agency subject to the requirements of this section shall annually report to Congress regarding its compliance with such requirements, including a tabulation of the total number of agency meetings open to the public, the total number of meetings closed to the public, the reasons for closing such meetings, and a description of any litigation brought against the agency under this section, including any costs assessed against the agency in such litigation (whether or not paid by the agency),

k) Nothing herein expands or limits the present rights of any person under section 552 of this title, except that the exemptions set forth in subsection (c) of this section shall govern in the case of any request made pursuant to section 552 to copy or inspect the transcripts, recordings, or minutes described in subsection (f) of this section. The requirements of chapter 33 of title 44, United States Code, shall not apply to the transcripts, recordings, and minutes described in subsection (f) of this section.

l) This section does not constitute authority to withhold any information from Congress, and does not authorize the closing of any agency meeting or portion thereof required by any other provision of law to be open.

m) Nothing in this section authorizes any agency to withhold from any individual any record, including transcripts, recordings, or minutes required by this section, which is otherwise accessible to such individual under section 552a of this title.

§ 553. Rule making

a) This section applies, according to the provisions thereof, except to the extent that there is involved -

1) a military or foreign affairs function of the United States; or
2) a matter relating to agency management or personnel or to public property, loans, grants, benefits, or contracts.

b) General notice of proposed rule making shall be published in the Federal Register, unless persons subject thereto are named and either personally served or otherwise have actual notice thereof in accordance with law. The notice shall include -

1) a statement of the time, place, and nature of public rule making proceedings;
2) reference to the legal authority under which the rule is proposed; and
3) either the terms or substance of the proposed rule or a description of the subjects and issues involved,

   Except when notice or hearing is required by statute, this subsection does not apply -
   A) to interpretative rules, general statements of policy, or rules of agency organization, procedure, or practice; or

B) when the agency for good cause finds (and incorporates the finding and a brief statement of reasons therefore in the rules issued) that notice and public procedure thereon are impracticable, unnecessary, or contrary to the public interest.

c) After notice required by this section, the agency shall give interested persons an opportunity to participate in the rule making through submission of written data, views, or arguments with or without opportunity for oral presentation. After consideration of the relevant matter presented, the agency shall incorporate in the rules adopted a concise general statement of their basis and purpose. When rules are required by statute to be made on the record after opportunity for an agency hearing, sections 556 and 557 of this title apply instead of this subsection.

d) The required publication or service of a substantive rule shall be made not less than 30 days before its effective date, except -

1) a substantive rule which grants or recognizes an exemption or relieves a restriction;
2) interpretative rules and statements of policy; or
3) as otherwise provided by the agency for good cause found and published with the rule.

e) Each agency shall give an interested person the right to petition for the issuance, amendment, or repeal of a rule.

§ 554. Adjudications

a) This section applies, according to the provisions thereof in every case of adjudication required by statute to be determined on the record after opportunity for an agency hearing, except to the extent that there is involved -

1) a matter subject to a subsequent trial of the law and the facts de novo in a court;
2) the selection or tenure of an employee, except an administrative law judge appointed under section 3105 of this title;
3) proceedings in which decisions rest solely on inspections, tests, or elections;
4) the conduct of military or foreign affairs functions;
5) cases in which an agency is acting as an agent for a court; or

6) the certification of worker representatives.

b) Persons entitled to notice of an agency hearing shall be timely informed of-

1) the time, place, and nature of the hearing;
2) the legal authority and jurisdiction under which the hearing is to be held; and
3) the matters of fact and law asserted.

When private persons are the moving parties, other parties to the proceeding shall give prompt notice of issues controverted in fact or law; and in other instances agencies may by rule require responsive pleading. In fixing the time and place for hearings, due regard shall be had for the convenience and necessity of the parties or their representatives.

c) The agency shall give all interested parties opportunity for -

1) the submission and consideration of facts, arguments, offers of settlement, or proposals of adjustment when time, the nature of the proceeding, and the public interest permit; and
2) to the extent that the parties are unable so to determine a controversy by consent, hearing and decision on notice and in accordance with sections 556 and 557 of this title.

d) The employee who presides at the reception of evidence pursuant to section 556 of this title shall make the recommended decision or initial decision required by section 557 of this title, unless he becomes unavailable to the agency. Except to the extent required for the disposition of *ex parte* matters as authorized by law, such an employee may not -

1) consult a person or party on a fact in issue, unless on notice and opportunity for all parties to participate; or
2) be responsible to or subject to the supervision or direction of an employee or agent engaged in the performance of investigative or prosecuting functions for an agency.

An employee or agent engaged in the performance of investigative or prosecuting functions for an agency in a case may not, in that or a factually related case, participate or advise in the decision, recommended decision, or agency review pursuant to section 557 of this title, except as witness or counsel in public proceedings. This subsection does not apply -

A) in determining applications for initial licenses;
B) to proceedings involving the validity or application of rates, facilities, or practices of public utilities or carriers; or
C) to the agency or a member or members of the body comprising the agency.

e) The agency, with like effect as in the case of other orders, and in its sound discretion, may issue a declaratory order to terminate a controversy or remove uncertainty.

§ 555. Ancillary matters

a) This section applies, according to the provisions thereof, except as otherwise provided by this subchapter.
b) A person compelled to appear in person before an agency or representative thereof is entitled to be accompanied, represented, and advised by counsel or, if permitted by the agency, by other qualified representative. A party is entitled to appear in person or by or with counsel or other duly qualified representative in an agency proceeding. So far as the orderly conduct of public business permits, an interested person may appear before an agency or its responsible employees for the presentation, adjustment, or determination of an issue, request, or controversy in a proceeding, whether interlocutory, summary, or otherwise, or in connection with an agency function. With due regard for the convenience and necessity of the parties or their representatives and within a reasonable time, each agency shall proceed to conclude a matter presented to it. This subsection does not grant or deny a person who is not a lawyer the right to appear for or represent others before an agency or in an agency proceeding.
c) Process, requirement of a report, inspection, or other investigative act or demand may not be issued, made, or enforced except as authorized by law. A person compelled to submit data or evidence is entitled to retain or, on payment of lawfully prescribed costs, procure a copy or transcript thereof, except that in a nonpublic investigatory proceeding the witness may for good cause be limited to inspection of the official transcript of his testimony.

d) Agency subpoenas authorized by law shall be issued to a party on request and, when required by rules of procedure, on a statement or showing of general relevance and reasonable scope of the evidence sought. On contest, the court shall sustain the subpoena or similar process or demand to the extent that it is found to be in accordance with law. In a proceeding for enforcement, the court shall issue an order requiring the appearance of the witness or the production of the evidence or data within a reasonable time under penalty of punishment for contempt in cases of contumacious failure to comply.

e) Prompt notice shall be given of the denial in whole or in part of a written application, petition, or other request of an interested person made in connection with any agency proceeding. Except in affirming a prior denial or when the denial is self-explanatory, the notice shall be accompanied by a brief statement of the grounds for denial.

§ 556. Hearings; presiding employees; powers and duties; burden of proof; evidence; record as basis of decision

a) This section applies, according to the provisions thereof, to hearings required by section 553 or 554 of this title to be conducted in accordance with this section.

b) There shall preside at the taking of evidence -

   1) the agency;

   2) one or more members of the body which comprises the agency; or

   3) one or more administrative law judges appointed under section 3105 of this title.

   This subchapter does not supersede the conduct of specified classes of proceedings, in whole or in part, by or before boards or other employees specially provided for by or designated under statute. The functions of presiding employees and of employees participating in decisions in accordance with section 557 of this title shall be conducted in an impartial manner. A presiding or participating employee may at any time disqualify himself. On the filing in good faith of a timely and sufficient affidavit of personal bias or other disqualification of a presiding or participating employee, the agency shall determine the matters as a part of the record and decision in the case.

c) Subject to published rules of the agency and within its powers, employees presiding at hearings may -

1) administer oaths and affirmations;
2) issue subpoenas authorized by law;
3) rule on offers of proof and receive relevant evidence;
4) take depositions or have depositions taken when the ends of justice would be served;
5) regulate the course of the hearing;
6) hold conferences for the settlement or simplification of the issues by consent of the parties;
7) dispose of procedural requests or similar matters;
8) make or recommend decisions in accordance with section 557 of this title; and
9) take other action authorized by agency rule consistent with this subchapter.

d) Except as otherwise provided by statute, the proponent of a rule or order has the burden of proof. Any oral or documentary evidence may be received, but the agency as a matter of policy shall provide for the exclusion of irrelevant, immaterial, or unduly repetitious evidence. A sanction may not be imposed or rule or order issued except on consideration of the whole record or those parts thereof cited by a party and supported by and in accordance with the reliable, probative, and substantial evidence. The agency may, to the extent consistent with the interests of justice and the policy of the underlying statutes administered by the agency, consider a violation of section 557(d) of this title sufficient grounds for a decision adverse to a party who has knowingly committed such violation or knowingly caused such violation to occur. A party is entitled to present his case or defense by oral or documentary evidence, to submit rebuttal evidence, and to conduct such cross-examination as may be required for a full and true disclosure of the facts. In rule making or determining claims for money or benefits or applications for initial licenses an agency may, when a party will not be prejudiced thereby, adopt procedures for the submission of all or part of the evidence in written form.

e) The transcript of testimony and exhibits, together with all papers and requests filed in the proceeding, constitutes the exclusive record for decision in accordance with section 557 of this title and, on payment of lawfully prescribed costs, shall be made available to the parties. When an agency decision rests on official notice of a material fact not appearing in the evidence in the record, a party is entitled, on timely request, to an opportunity to show the contrary.

§ 557. Initial decisions; conclusiveness; review by agency; submissions by parties; contents of decisions; record

a)   This section applies, according to the provisions thereof, when a hearing is required to be conducted in accordance with section 556 of this title.

b)   When the agency did not preside at the reception of the evidence, the presiding employee or, in cases not subject to section 554(d) of this title, an employee qualified to preside at hearings pursuant to section 556 of this title, shall initially decide the case unless the agency requires, either in specific cases *or* by general rule, the entire record to be certified to it for decision. When the presiding employee makes an initial decision, that decision then becomes the decision of the agency without further proceedings unless there is an appeal to, *or* review on motion of, the agency within time provided by rule. On appeal from or review of the initial decision, the agency has all the powers which it would have in making the initial decision except as it may limit the issues on notice or by rule. When the agency makes the decision without having presided at the reception of the evidence, the presiding employee or an employee qualified to preside at hearings pursuant to section 556 of this title shall first recommend a decision, except that in rule making or determining application for initial licenses -

1)   instead thereof the agency may issue a tentative decision or one of its responsible employees may recommend a decision; or

2)   this procedure may be omitted in a case in which the agency finds on the record that due and timely execution of its functions imperatively and unavoidably so requires.

c)   Before a recommended, initial, or tentative decision, or a decision on agency review of the decision of subordinate employees, the parties are entitled to a reasonable opportunity to submit for the consideration of the employees participating in the decisions -

1) proposed findings and conclusions; or

2) exceptions to the decisions or recommended decisions of subordinate employees or to tentative agency decisions; and

3) supporting reasons for the exceptions or proposed findings *or* conclusions.

The record shall show the ruling on each finding, conclusion, or exception presented. All decisions, including initial, recommended, and tentative decisions, are a part of the record and shall include a statement of -

A) findings and conclusions, and the reasons or basis therefore, on all the material issues of fact, law, or discretion presented on the record; and

B) the appropriate rule, order, sanction, relief, or denial thereof.

d) (1) In any agency proceeding which is subject to subsection (a) of this section, except to the extent required for the disposition of *ex parte* matters as authorized by law -

A) no interested person outside the agency shall make or knowingly cause to be made to any member of the body comprising the agency, administrative law judge, or other employee who is or may reasonably be expected to be involved in the decisional process of the proceeding, an *ex parte* communication relevant to the merits of the proceeding;

B) no member of the body comprising the agency, administrative law judge, or other employee who is or may reasonably be expected to be involved in the decisional process of the proceeding, shall make or knowingly cause to be made to any interested person outside the agency an *ex parte* communication relevant to the merits of the proceeding;

C) a member of the body comprising the agency, administrative law judge, or other employee who is or may reasonably be expected to be involved in the decisional process of such proceeding who receives, or who makes *or* knowingly causes to be made, a communication prohibited by this subsection shall place

on the public record of the proceeding:
    i.   all such written communications;
    ii.   memoranda stating the substance of all such oral communications; and
    iii. all written responses, and memoranda stating the substance of all oral responses, to the materials described in clauses (i) and (ii) of this subparagraph;

D) upon receipt of a communication knowingly made or knowingly caused to be made by a party in violation of this subsection, the agency, administrative law judge, or other employee presiding at the hearing may, to the extent consistent with the interests of justice and the policy of the underlying statutes, require the party to show cause why his claim or interest in the proceeding should not be dismissed, denied, disregarded, or otherwise adversely affected on account of such violation; and

E) the prohibitions of this subsection shall apply beginning at such time as the agency may designate, but in no case shall they begin to apply later than the time at which a proceeding is noticed for hearing unless the person responsible for the communication has knowledge that it will be noticed, in which case the prohibitions shall apply beginning at the time of his acquisition of such knowledge.

2) This subsection does not constitute authority to withhold information from Congress.

§ 558. Imposition of sanctions; determination of applications for licenses; suspension, revocation, and expiration of licenses

a) This section applies, according to the provisions thereof, to the exercise of a power or authority.

b) A sanction may not be imposed or a substantive rule or order issued except within jurisdiction delegated to the agency and as authorized by law.

c) When application is made for a license required by law, the agency, with due regard for the rights and privileges of all the interested parties or adversely affected persons and within a reasonable time, shall set and complete proceedings required to be conducted in accordance with sections 556 and 557 of this title or other proceedings required by law and shall make its decision. Except in cases of willfulness or those in which public health, interest, or safety requires otherwise, the withdrawal, suspension, revocation, or annulment of a license is lawful only if, before the institution of agency proceedings therefore, the licensee has been given -

1) notice by the agency in writing of the facts *or* conduct which may warrant the action; and
2) opportunity *to* demonstrate *or* achieve compliance with all lawful requirements.

> When the licensee has made timely and sufficient application for a renewal or a new license in accordance with agency rules, a license with reference *to an* activity of a continuing nature does not expire until the application has been finally determined by the agency.

§ 559. Effect on other laws; effect of subsequent statute

This subchapter, chapter 7, and sections 1305, 3105, 3344, 4301(2) (E), 5362, and 7521 of this title, and the provisions of section 5335 (a) (B) of this title that relate *to* administrative law judges, do not limit or repeal additional requirements imposed by statute or otherwise recognized by law. Except as otherwise required by law, requirements or privileges relating to evidence *or* procedure apply equally *to* agencies and persons. Each agency is granted the authority necessary to comply with the requirements of this subchapter through the issuance of rules *or* otherwise. Subsequent statute may not be held to supersede or modify this subchapter, chapter 7, sections 1305, 3105, 3344, 4301(2) (E), 5362, or 7521, or the provisions of section 5335(a) (B) of this title that relate to administrative law judges, except to the extent that it does so expressly.

§ 701. Application; definitions

a) This chapter applies, according to the provisions thereof, except to the extent that -

1) statutes preclude judicial review; or
2) agency action is committed to agency discretion by law.

b) For the purpose of this chapter -

1) agency means each authority of the Government of the United States, whether or not it is within or subject to review by another agency, but does not include -

A) the Congress;
B) the courts of the United States;
C) the governments of the territories or possessions of the United States;
D) the government of the District of Columbia;
E) agencies composed of representatives of the parties or of representatives of organizations of the parties to the disputes determined by them;
F) courts martial and military commissions;
G) military authority exercised in the field in time of war or in occupied territory; or
H) functions conferred by sections 1738,1739, 1743, and 1744 of title 12; chapter 2 of title 41; or sections 1622,1884, 1891-1902, and former section 1641(b) (2), of title 50, appendix; and

2) "person," "rule," "order," "license," "sanction," "relief," and "agency action" have the meanings given them by section 551 of this title.

§ 702. Right of review

A person suffering legal wrong because of agency action, or adversely affected or aggrieved by agency action within the meaning of a relevant statute, is entitled to judicial review thereof. An action in a court of the United States seeking relief other than money damages and stating a claim that an agency or an officer or employee thereof acted or failed to act in an official capacity or under color of legal authority shall not be dismissed nor relief therein be denied on the ground that it is against the United States or that the United States is an indispensable party. The United States may be named as a defendant in any such action, and a judgment or decree may be entered against the United States: *Provided,* That any mandatory or injunctive decree shall specify the Federal officer or officers (by name or by title), and their successors in office, personally responsible for compliance. Nothing herein (1) affects other limitations on judicial review or the power or duty of the court to dismiss any action or deny relief on any other appropriate legal or equitable ground; or (2) confers authority to grant relief if any other statute that grants consent to suit expressly or impliedly forbids the relief which is sought.

§ 703. Form and venue of proceeding

The form of proceeding for judicial review is the special statutory review proceeding relevant to the subject matter in a court specified by statute or, in the absence or inadequacy thereof, any applicable form of legal action, including actions for declaratory judgments or writs of prohibitory or mandatory injunction or habeas corpus, in a court of competent jurisdiction. If no special statutory review proceeding is applicable, the action for judicial review may be brought against the United States, the agency by its official title, or the appropriate officer. Except to the extent that prior, adequate, and exclusive opportunity for judicial review is provided by law, agency action is subject to judicial review in civil or criminal proceedings for judicial enforcement.

§ 704. Actions reviewable

Agency action made reviewable by statute and final agency action for which there is no other adequate remedy in a court are subject to judicial review. A preliminary, procedural, or intermediate agency action or ruling not directly reviewable is subject to review on the review of the final agency action. Except as otherwise expressly required by statute, agency action otherwise final is final for the purposes of this section whether or not there has been presented *or* determined an application for a declaratory order, for any form of reconsideration, or, unless the agency otherwise requires by rule and provides that the action meanwhile is inoperative, for an appeal to superior agency authority.

§ 705. Relief pending review

When an agency finds that justice so requires, it may postpone the effective date of action taken by it, pending judicial review. On such conditions as may be required and to the extent necessary to prevent irreparable injury, the reviewing court, including the court to which a case may be taken on appeal from or on application for certiorari or other writ to a reviewing court, may issue all necessary and appropriate process to postpone the effective date of an agency action or to preserve status or rights pending conclusion of the review proceedings.

§ 706. Scope of review

To the extent necessary to decision and when presented, the reviewing court shall decide all relevant questions of law, interpret constitutional and statutory provisions, and determine the meaning or applicability of the terms of an agency action. The reviewing court shall -

1) compel agency action unlawfully withheld or unreasonably delayed; and
2) hold unlawful and set aside agency action, findings, and conclusions found to be -
   A) arbitrary, capricious, an abuse of discretion, or otherwise not in accordance with law;
   B) contrary to constitutional right, power, privilege, or immunity;
   C) in excess of statutory jurisdiction, authority, or limitations, or short of statutory right;
   D) without observance of procedure required by law;
   E) unsupported by substantial evidence in a case subject to section 556 and 557 of this title or otherwise reviewed on the record of an agency hearing provided by statute; or
   F) unwarranted by the facts to the extent that the facts are subject to trial de novo by the reviewing court.

   In making the foregoing determinations, the court shall review the whole record or those parts of it cited by the party, and due account shall be taken of the rule of prejudicial error.

§ 3105. Appointment of administrative law judges

Each agency shall appoint as many administrative law judges as are necessary for proceedings required to be conducted in accordance with sections 556 and 557 of this title. Administrative law judges shall be assigned to cases in rotation so far as practicable, and may not perform duties inconsistent with their duties and responsibilities as administrative law judges.

a) An action may be taken against an administrative law judge appointed under section 3105 of this title by the agency in which the administrative law judge is employed only for good cause established and determined by the Merit Systems Protection Board on the record after opportunity for hearing before the Board.

b) The actions covered by this section are -
    1) a removal;
    2) a suspension;
    3) a reduction in grade;
    4) a reduction in pay; and
    5) a furlough of 30 days or less; but do not include -

        A) a suspension or removal [in the interest of a national security};
        B) a reduction-in-force action . . .; or
        C) any action initiated [by the Special Counsel of the Board].

§ 5372. Administrative law judges

Administrative law judges appointed under section 3105 of this title are entitled to pay prescribed by the Office of Personnel Management independently of agency recommendations or ratings and in accordance with subchapter III of this chapter and chapter 51 of this title.

§ 3344. Details, administrative law judges

An agency as defined by section 551 of this title which occasionally or temporarily is insufficiently staffed with administrative law judges appointed under section 3105 of this title may use administrative law judges selected by the Office of Personnel Management from and with the consent of other agencies.

§ 1305. Administrative law judges

For the purpose of sections 3105, 3344, 4301(2) (E), 5362, and 7521 and the provisions of section 5335 (a) (B) of this title that relate to administrative law judges, the Office of Personnel Management may investigate, and for the purpose of section 7521 of this title, the Merit System Protection Board require reports by agencies, issue reports, including an annual report to Congress, prescribe regulations, appoint advisory committees as necessary, recommend legislation, subpoena witnesses and records, and pay witness fees as established for the courts of the United States.

IX. Uniform Law Commissioners' Revised Model State Administrative Procedure Act, 1970 Version

Concerns Procedure of State Administrative Agencies and Review of Their Determinations.
[Be it enacted ....]

SECTION 1. *[Definitions.]* As used in this Act:
1) "agency" means each state [board, commission, department, *or* officer], other than the legislature or the courts, authorized by law to make rules or to determine contested cases;
2) "contested case" means a proceeding, including but not restricted to ratemaking, [price fixing], and licensing, in which the legal rights, duties, or privileges of a party are required by law to be determined by an agency after an opportunity for hearing;
3) "license" includes the whole or part of any agency permit, certificate, approval, registration, charter, or similar form of permission required by law, but it does not include a license required solely for revenue purposes;
4) "licensing" includes the agency process respecting the grant, denial, renewal, revocation, suspension, annulment, withdrawal, or amendment of a license;
5) "party" means each person or agency named or admitted as a party, or properly seeking and entitled as of right to be admitted as a party;
6) "person" means any individual, partnership, corporation, association, governmental subdivision, or public or private organization of any character other than an agency;
7) "rule" means each agency statement of general applicability that implements, interprets, or prescribes law or policy, or describes the organization, procedure, or practice requirements of any agency. The term includes the amendment or repeal of a prior rule, but does not include (A) statements concerning only the internal management of an agency and not affecting private rights or procedures

available to the public, or (B) declaratory rulings issued pursuant to Section 8, or (C) intra-agency memoranda.

SECTION 2. *[Public In formation; Adoption of Rules; Availability of Rules and Orders.*

a) In addition to other rule-making requirements imposed by law, each agency shall:

   1) adopt as a rule a description of its organization, stating the general course and method of its operations and the methods whereby the public may obtain information or make submissions or requests;

   2) adopt rules of practice setting forth the nature, and requirements of all formal and informal procedures available, including a description of all forms and instructions used by the agency;

   3) make available for public inspection all rules and all other written statements of policy or interpretations formulated, adopted, or used by the agency in the discharge of its functions;

   4) make available for public inspection all final orders, decisions, and opinions.

b) No agency rule, order, or decision is valid or effective against any person *or* party, nor may it be invoked by the agency for any purpose, until it has been made available for public inspection as herein required. This provision is not applicable in favor of any person or party who has actual knowledge thereof.

SECTION 3. *[Procedure for Adoption of Rules.]*

a) Prior to the adoption, amendment, or repeal of any rule, the agency shall:

   1) give at least 20 days' notice of its intended action. The notice shall include a statement of either the terms or substance of the intended action or a description of the subjects and issues involved, and the time when, the place where, and the manner in which interested persons may present their views thereon. The notice shall be mailed to all persons who have made timely request of the agency for advance notice of its rule-making proceedings and shall be published in [here insert the medium of publication appropriate for the adopting state];

2) afford all interested persons reasonable opportunity to submit data, views, or arguments, orally or in writing. In case of substantive rules, opportunity for oral hearing must be granted if requested by 25 persons, by a governmental subdivision or agency, or by an association having not less than 25 members. The agency shall consider fully all written and oral submissions respecting the proposed rule. Upon adoption of a rule, the agency, if requested to do so by an interested person either prior to adoption or within 30 days thereafter, shall issue a concise statement of the principal reasons for and against its adoption, incorporating therein its reasons for overruling the considerations urged against its adoption.

b) If an agency finds that an imminent peril to the public health, safety, or welfare requires adoption of a rule upon fewer than 20 days' notice and states in writing its reasons for that finding, it may proceed without prior notice or hearing or upon any abbreviated notice and hearing that it finds practicable, to adopt an emergency rule. The rule may be effective for a period of not longer than 120 days [renewable once for a period not exceeding days], but the adoption of an identical rule under subsections (a) (1) and (a) (2) of this Section is not precluded.

c) No rule hereafter adopted is valid unless adopted in substantial compliance with this Section. A proceeding to contest any rule on the ground of non-compliance with the procedural requirements of this Section must be commenced within 2 years from the effective date of the rule.

SECTION 4. *[Filing and Taking Effect of Rules.]*

a) Each agency shall file in the office of the [Secretary of State] a certified copy of each rule adopted by it, including all rules existing on the effective date of this Act. The [Secretary of State] shall keep a permanent register of the rules open to public inspection.

b) Each rule hereafter adopted is effective 20 days after filing, except that:

1) if a later date is required by statute or specified in the rule, the later date is the effective date;

2) subject to applicable constitutional or statutory provisions, an emergency rule becomes effective immediately upon

filing with the [Secretary of State], or at a stated date less than 20 days thereafter, if the agency finds that this effective date is necessary because of imminent peril to the public health, safety, or welfare. The agency's finding and a brief statement of the reasons therefore shall be filed with the rule. The agency shall take appropriate measures to make emergency rules known to the persons who ma)' be affected by

SECTION 5. *[Publication of Rules.]*
a) The [Secretary of State] shall compile, index, and publish all effective rules adopted by each agency. Compilations shall be supplemented or revised as often as necessary [and at least once every 2 years].
b) The [Secretary of State] shall publish a [monthly] bulletin setting forth the text of all rules filed during the preceding [month] excluding rules in effect upon the adoption of this Act.
c) The [Secretary of State] may omit from the bulletin or compilation any rule the publication of which would be unduly cumbersome, expensive, or otherwise inexpedient, if the rule in printed or processed form is made available on application to the adopting agency, and if the bulletin or compilation contains a notice stating the general subject matter of the omitted rule and stating how a copy thereof may be obtained.
d) Bulletins and compilations shall be made available upon request to [agencies and officials of this State] free of charge and to other persons at prices fixed by the [Secretary of State] to cover mailing and publication costs.

SECTION 6. *[Petition for Adoption of Rules.]* An interested person may petition an agency requesting the promulgation, amendment, or repeal of a rule. Each agency shall prescribe by rule the form for petitions and the procedure for their submission, consideration, and disposition. Within 30 days after submission of a petition, the agency either shall deny the petition in writing (stating its reasons for the denials) or shall initiate rule-making proceedings in accordance with Section 3.

SECTION 7. *[Declaratory Judgment on Validity or Applicability of Rules.]* The validity or applicability of a rule may be determined in an action for declaratory judgment in the [District Court of. .. County], if it is alleged that the rule, or its threatened application, interferes with or impairs, or threatens to interfere with or impair, the legal rights or privileges of the plaintiff. The agency shall be made a party to the action. A declaratory judgment may be rendered whether or not the plaintiff has requested the agency to pass upon the validity or applicability of the rule in question.

SECTION 8. *[Declaratory Rulings by Agencies.]* Each agency shall provide by rule for the filing and prompt disposition of petitions for declaratory rulings as to the applicability of any statutory provision or of any rule or order of the agency. Rulings disposing of petitions have the same status as agency decisions or orders in contested cases.

SECTION 9. *[Contested Cases; Notice; Hearing; Records.]*
a) In a contested case, all parties shall be afforded an opportunity for hearing after reasonable notice.
b) The notice shall include:

    1) a statement of the time, place, and nature of the hearing;
    2) a statement of the legal authority and jurisdiction under which the hearing is to be held;
    3) a reference to the particular sections of the statutes and rules involved;
    4) a short and plain statement of the matters asserted. If the agency or other party is unable to state the matters in detail at the time the notice is served, the initial notice may be limited to a statement of the issues involved. Thereafter upon application a more definite and detailed statement shall be furnished.

c) Opportunity shall be afforded all parties to respond and present evidence and argument on all issues involved.
d) Unless precluded by law, informal disposition may be made of any contested case by stipulation, agreed settlement, consent order, or default.
e) The record in a contested case shall include:

    1) all pleadings, motions, intermediate rulings;
    2) evidence received or considered;
    3) a statement of matters officially noticed;
    4) questions and offers of proof, objections, and rulings thereon;
    5) proposed findings and exceptions;
    6) any decision, opinion, or report by the officer presiding at the hearing;
    7) all staff memoranda or data submitted to the hearing officer or members of the agency in connection with their

consideration of the case.

f) Oral proceedings or any part thereof shall be transcribed on request of any party.

g) Findings of fact shall be based exclusively on the evidence and on matters officially noticed.

SECTION 10. *[Rules of Evidence; Official Notice.]* In contested cases:

1) irrelevant, immaterial, or unduly repetitious evidence shall be excluded. The rules of evidence as applied in [nonjury] civil cases in the [District Courts of this State] shall be followed. When necessary to ascertain facts not reasonably susceptible of proof under those rules, evidence not admissible there under may be admitted (except where precluded by statute) if it is of a type commonly relied upon by reasonably prudent men in the conduct of their affairs. Agencies shall give effect to the rules of privilege recognized by law. Objections to evidentiary offers may be made and shall be noted in the record. Subject to these requirements, when a hearing will be expedited and the interests of the parties will not be prejudiced substantially, any part of the evidence may be received in written form;

2) documentary evidence may be received in the form of copies or excerpts, if the original is not readily available. Upon request, parties shall be given an opportunity to compare the copy with the original;

3) a party may conduct cross-examinations required for a full and true disclosure of the facts;

4) notice may be taken of judicially cognizable facts. In addition, notice may be taken of generally recognized technical or scientific facts within the agency's specialized knowledge. Parties shall be notified either before or during the hearing, or by reference in preliminary reports or otherwise, of the material noticed, including any staff memoranda or data, and they shall be afforded an opportunity to contest the material so noticed. The agency's experience, technical competence, and specialized knowledge may be utilized in the evaluation of the evidence.

SECTION 11. *[Examination of Evidence by Agency.]* When in a contested case a majority of the officials of the agency who are to render the final decision have not heard the case or read the record, the decision, if adverse to a party to the proceeding other than the agency itself, shall not be made until a proposal for decision is served upon the parties, and an opportunity is afforded to each party adversely affected to file exceptions and present briefs and oral argument to the officials who are to render the decision. The proposal for decision shall contain a `statement of the reasons therefore and of each issue of fact or law necessary to the proposed decision, prepared by the person who conducted the hearing or one who has read the record. The parties by written stipulation may waive compliance with this section.

SECTION 12. *[Decisions and Orders.]* A final decision or order adverse to a party in a contested case shall be in writing or stated in the record. A final decision shall include findings of fact and conclusions of law, separately stated. Findings   of fact, if set forth in statutory language, shall be accompanied by a concise and explicit statement of the underlying facts supporting the findings. If, in accordance with agency rules, a party submitted proposed findings of fact, the decision shall include a ruling upon each proposed finding. Parties shall be notified either personally or by mail of any decision or order. Upon request a copy of the decision or order shall be delivered or mailed forthwith to each party and to his attorney of record.

SECTION 13. *[Ex Parte Consultations.]* Unless required for the disposition of *ex parte* matters authorized by law, members or employees of an agency assigned to render a decision or to make findings of fact and conclusions of law in a contested case shall not communicate, directly or indirectly, in connection with any issue of fact, with any person or party, nor, in connection with any issue of law, with any party or his representative, except upon notice and opportunity for all parties to participate. An agency member
1) may communicate with other members of the agency, and
2) may have the aid and advice of one or more personal assistants.

SECTION 14. *[Licenses.]*
a) When the grant, denial, or renewal of a license is required to be preceded by notice and opportunity for hearing, the provisions of this Act concerning contested cases apply.
b) When a licensee has made timely and sufficient application for the renewal of a license or a new license with reference to any activity of a continuing nature, the existing license does not

expire until the application has been finally determined by the agency, and, in case the application is denied or the terms of the new license limited, until the last day for seeking review of the agency order or a later date fixed by order of the reviewing court.

c) No revocation, suspension, annulment, or withdrawal of any license is lawful unless, prior to the institution of agency proceedings, the agency gave notice by mail to the licensee of facts or conduct which warrant the intended action, and the licensee was given an opportunity to show compliance with all lawful requirements for the retention of the license. If the agency finds that public health, safety, or welfare imperatively requires emergency action, and incorporates a finding to that effect in its order, summary suspension of a license may be ordered pending proceedings for revocation or other action. These proceedings shall be promptly instituted and determined.

SECTION 15. *[Judicial Review of Contested Cases.]*

a) A person who has exhausted all administrative remedies available within the agency and who is aggrieved by a final decision in a contested case is entitled to judicial review under this Act. This Section does not limit utilization of or the scope of judicial review available under other means of review, redress, relief, or trial *de novo* provided by law. A preliminary, procedural, or intermediate agency action or ruling is immediately reviewable if review of the final agency decision would not provide an adequate remedy.

b) Proceedings for review are instituted by filing a petition in the [District Court of the County] within [30] days after [mailing notice of] the final decision of the agency or, if a rehearing is requested, within [30] days after the decision thereon. Copies of the petition shall be served upon the agency and all parties of record.

c) The filing of the petition does not itself stay enforcement of the agency decision. The agency may grant, or the reviewing court may order, a stay upon appropriate terms.

d) Within [30] days after the service of the petition, or within further time allowed by the court, the agency shall transmit to the reviewing court the original or a certified copy of the entire record of the proceeding under review. By stipulation of all parties to the review proceedings, the record may be shortened. A party unreasonably refusing to stipulate to limit the record may be taxed by the court for the additional costs. The court may require or permit subsequent corrections or additions to the record.

e) If, before the date set for hearing, application is made to the court for leave to present additional evidence, and it is shown to the satisfaction of the court that the additional evidence is material and that there were good reasons for failure to present it in the proceeding before the agency, the court may order that the additional evidence be taken before the agency upon conditions determined by the court. The agency may modify its findings and decision by reason of the additional evidence and shall file that evidence and any modifications, new findings, or decisions with the reviewing court.

f) The review shall be conducted by the court without a jury and shall be confined to the record. In cases of alleged irregularities in procedure before the agency, not shown in the record, proof thereon may be taken in the court. The court, upon request, shall hear oral argument and receive written briefs.

g) The court shall not substitute its judgment for that of the agency as to the weight of the evidence on questions of fact. The court may affirm the decision of the agency or remand the case for further proceedings. The court may reverse or modify the decision if substantial rights of the appellant have been prejudiced because the administrative findings, inferences, conclusions, or decisions are:

1) in violation of constitutional or statutory provisions;
2) in excess of the statutory authority of the agency;
3) made upon unlawful procedure;
4) affected by other error of law;
5) clearly erroneous in view of the reliable, probative, and substantial evidence on the whole record; or
6) arbitrary or capricious or characterized by abuse of discretion or clearly unwarranted exercise of discretion.

SECTION 16. *[Appeals.]* An aggrieved party may obtain a review of any final judgment of the [District Court] under this Act by appeal to the [Supreme Court]. The appeal shall be taken as in other civil cases.

SECTION 17. *[Severability.]* If any provision of this Act or the application thereof to any person or circumstance is held invalid, the invalidity does not affect other provisions or applications of the Act which can be given effect without the invalid provision or application, and for this purpose the provisions of this Act are severable.

SECTION 18. *[repeal]* *The* following acts and parts of acts are repealed:

SECTION 19. *[Time of Taking Effect and Scope of Application.]* This Act takes effect and (except as to proceedings then pending) applies to all agencies and agency proceedings not expressly exempted.

X. REGULATORY FLEXIBILITY ACT

PUBLIC LAW 96-354 [S. 299]; September 19, 1980

An Act to amend title 5, United States Code to improve Federal rulemaking by creating procedures to analyze the availability of more flexible regulatory approaches for small entities, and for other purposes.

Be it enacted by the Senate and House of Representatives of the United States of America in Congress assembled, That this Act may be cited as the "Regulatory Flexibility Act."

FINDINGS AND PURPOSES

SEC. 2.

a) The Congress finds and declares that-

1) when adopting regulations to protect the health, safety and economic welfare of the Nation, Federal agencies should seek to achieve statutory goals as effectively and efficiently as possible without imposing unnecessary burdens on the public;

2) laws and regulations designed for application to large scale entities have been applied uniformly to small businesses, small organizations, and small governmental jurisdictions even though the problems that gave rise to government action may not have been caused by those smaller entities;

3) uniform Federal regulatory and reporting requirements have in numerous instances imposed unnecessary and disproportionately burdensome demands including legal, accounting and consulting costs upon small businesses, small organizations, and small governmental jurisdictions with limited resources;

4) the failure to recognize differences in the scale and resources of regulated entities has in numerous instances adversely affected competition in the marketplace, discouraged innovation and restricted improvements in productivity;

5) unnecessary regulations create entry barriers in many industries and discourage potential entrepreneurs from

introducing beneficial products and processes;

6) the practice of treating all regulated businesses, organizations, and governmental jurisdictions as equivalent may lead to inefficient use of regulatory agency resources, enforcement problems, and, in some cases, to actions inconsistent with the legislative intent of health, safety, environmental and economic welfare legislation;

7) alternative regulatory approaches which do not conflict with the stated objectives of applicable statutes may be available which minimize the significant economic impact of rules on small businesses, small organizations, and small governmental jurisdictions;

8) the process by which Federal regulations are developed and adopted should be reformed to require agencies to solicit the ideas and comments of small businesses, small organizations, and small governmental jurisdictions to examine the impact of proposed and existing rules on such entities, and to review the continued need for existing rules.

b) It is the purpose of this Act to establish as a principle of regulatory issuance that agencies shall endeavor, consistent with the objectives of the rule and of applicable statutes, to fit regulatory and informational requirements to the scale of the businesses, organizations, and governmental jurisdictions subject to regulation. To achieve this principle, agencies are required to solicit and consider flexible regulatory proposals and to explain the rationale for their actions to assure that such proposals are given serious consideration.

Analysis or Regulatory Functions

SEC. 3. (a) Title 5, United States Code, is amended by adding immediately after chapter 5 the following new chapter:

"CHAPTER 6"

THE ANALYSIS OF REGULATORY FUNCTIONS

§ 601. Definitions

"For purposes of this chapter -
1) the term 'agency' means an agency as defined in section 551(1) of this title;
2) the term 'rule' means any rule for which the agency publishes a general notice of proposed rulemaking pursuant to section 553(b) of this title, or any other law, including any rule of general applicability governing Federal grants to State and local governments for which the agency provides an opportunity for notice and public comment, except that the term 'rule' does not include a rule of particular applicability relating to rates, wages, corporate or financial structures or reorganizations thereof, prices, facilities, appliances, services, or allowances therefore or to valuations, costs or accounting, or practices relating to such rates, wages, structures, prices, appliances, services, or allowances;

3) the term 'small business' has the same meaning as the term 'small business concern under section 3 of the Small Business Act, unless an agency, after consultation with the Office of Advocacy of the Small Business Administration and after opportunity for public comment, establishes one or more definitions of such term which are appropriate to the activities of the agency and publishes such definition(s) in the Federal Register;

4) the term 'small organization' means any not-for-profit enterprise which is independently owned and operated and is not dominant in its field, unless an agency establishes, after opportunity for public comment, one or more definitions of such term which are appropriate to the activities of the agency and publishes such definition(s) in the Federal Register;

5) the term 'small governmental jurisdiction' means governments of cities, counties, towns, townships, villages, school districts, or special districts, with a population of less than fifty thousand, unless an agency establishes, after opportunity for public comment, one or more definitions of such term which are appropriate to the activities of the agency and which are based on such factors as location in rural or sparsely populated areas or limited revenues due to the population of such jurisdiction, and publishes such definition(s) in the Federal Register; and

6) the term 'small entity' shall have the same meaning as the terms 'small business', 'small organization' and 'small governmental jurisdiction' defined in paragraphs (3), (4) and (5) of this section.

§ 602. Regulatory agenda

a) During the months of October and April of each year, each agency shall publish in the Federal Register a regulatory flexibility agenda which shall contain

1) a brief description of the subject area of any rule which the agency expects to propose or promulgate which is likely to have a significant economic impact on a substantial number of small entities;

2) a summary of the nature of any such rule under consideration for each subject area listed in the agenda

pursuant to paragraph (1), the objectives and legal basis for the issuance of the rule, and an approximate schedule for completing action on any rule for which the agency has issued a general notice of proposed rulemaking, and

3) the name and telephone number of an agency official knowledgeable concerning the items listed in paragraph (1).

b) Each regulatory flexibility agenda shall be transmitted to the Chief Counsel for Advocacy of the Small Business Administration for comment, if any.

c) Each agency shall endeavor to provide notice of each regulatory flexibility agenda to small entities or their representatives through direct notification or publication of the agenda in publications likely to be obtained by such small entities and shall invite comments upon each subject area on the agenda.

d) Nothing in this section precludes an agency from considering or acting on any matter not included in a regulatory flexibility agenda, or requires an agency to consider or act on any matter listed in such agenda.

§ 603. Initial regulatory flexibility analysis

a) Whenever an agency is required by section 553 of this title, or any other law, to publish general notice of proposed rulemaking for any proposed rule, the agency shall prepare and make available for public comment an initial regulatory flexibility analysis. Such analysis shall describe the impact of the proposed rule on small entities. The initial regulatory flexibility analysis or a summary shall be published in the Federal Register at the time of the publication of general notice of proposed rulemaking for the rule. The agency shall transmit a copy of the initial regulatory flexibility analysis to the Chief Counsel for Advocacy of the Small Business Administration.

b) Each initial regulatory flexibility analysis required under this section shall contain -

1) a description of the reasons why action by the agency is being considered;

2) a succinct statement of the objectives of, and legal basis for, the proposed rule;

3) a description of and, where feasible, an estimate of the number of small entities to which the proposed rule will apply;

4) a description of the projected reporting, record keeping and other compliance requirements of the proposed rule, including an estimate of the classes of small entities which will be subject to the requirement and the type of professional skills necessary for preparation of the report or record;

5) an identification, to the extent practicable, of all relevant Federal rules which may duplicate, overlap or conflict with the proposed rule.

c) Each initial regulatory flexibility analysis shall also contain a description of any significant alternatives to the proposed rule which accomplish the stated objectives of applicable statutes and which minimize any significant economic impact of the proposed rule on small entities. Consistent with the stated objectives of applicable statutes, the analysis shall discuss significant alternatives such as -

1) the establishment of differing compliance or reporting requirements or timetables that take into account the resources available to small entities;

2) the clarification, consolidation, or simplification of compliance and reporting requirements under the rule for such small entities;

3) the use of performance rather than design standards; and

4) an exemption from coverage of the rule, or any part thereof, for such small entities.

§ 604. Final regulatory flexibility analysis

a) When an agency promulgates a final rule under section 553 of this title, after being required by that section or any other law to publish a general notice of proposed rulemaking, the agency shall prepare a final regulatory flexibility analysis. Each final regulatory flexibility analysis shall contain:

1) a succinct statement of the need for, and the objectives of, the rule;

2) a summary of the issues raised by the public comments in response to the initial regulatory flexibility analysis, a summary of the assessment of the agency of such issues, and a statement of any changes made in the proposed rule as a result of such comments; and

3) a description of each of the significant alternatives to the rule consistent with the stated objectives of applicable statutes and designed to minimize any significant economic impact of the rule on small entities which was considered by the agency, and a statement of the reasons why each one of such alternatives was rejected.

b) The agency shall make copies of the final regulatory flexibility analysis available to members of the public and shall publish in the Federal Register at the time of publication of the final rule under section 553 of this title a statement describing how the public may obtain such copies.

§ 605. Avoidance of duplicative or unnecessary analysis

a) Any Federal agency may perform the analyses required by sections 602, 603, and 604 of this title in conjunction with or as a part of any other agenda or analysis required by any other law if such other analysis satisfies the provisions of such sections.

b) Sections 603 and 604 of this title shall not apply to any proposed or final rule if the head of the agency certifies that the rule will not, if promulgated, have a significant economic impact on a substantial number of small entities. If the head of the agency makes a certification under the preceding sentence, the agency shall publish such certification in the Federal Register, at the time of publication of general notice of the proposed rulemaking for the rule or at the time of publication of the final rule, along with a succinct statement explaining the reasons for such certification, and provide such certification and statement to the Chief Counsel for Advocacy of the Small Business Administration.

c) In order to avoid duplicative action, an agency may consider a series of closely related rules as one rule for the purposes of sections 602,603, 604 and 610 of this title.

§ 606. Effect on other law

"The. requirements of sections 603 and 604 of this title do not alter in any manner standards otherwise applicable by law to agency action.

§ 607. Preparation of analyses

"In complying with the provisions of sections 603 and 604 of this title, an agency may provide either a quantifiable or numerical description of the effects of a proposed rule or alternatives to the proposed rule, or more general descriptive statements if quantification is not practicable or reliable.

§ 608. Procedure for waiver or delay of completion

a) An agency head may waive or delay the completion of some or all of the requirements of section 603 of this title by publishing in the Federal Register, not later than the date of publication of the final rule, a written finding, with reasons therefore, that the final rule is being promulgated in response to an emergency that makes compliance or timely compliance with the provisions of section 603 of this title impracticable.

b) Except as provided in section 605(b), an agency head may not waive the requirements of section 604 of this title. An agency head may delay the completion of the requirements of section 604 of this title for a period of not more than one hundred and eighty days after the date of publication in the Federal Register of a final rule by publishing in the Federal Register, not later than such date of publication, a written finding, with reasons therefore, that the final rule is being promulgated in response to an emergency that makes timely compliance with the provisions of section 604 of this title impracticable. If the agency has not prepared a final regulatory analysis pursuant to section 604 of this title within one hundred and eighty days from the date of publication of the final rule, such rule shall lapse and have no effect. Such rule shall not be repromulgated until a final regulatory flexibility analysis has been completed by the agency.

§ 609. Procedures for gathering comments

"When any rule is promulgated which will have a significant economic impact on a substantial number of small entities, the head of the agency promulgating the rule or the official of the agency with statutory responsibility for the promulgation of the rule shall assure that small entities have been given an opportunity to participate in the rulemaking for the rule through techniques such as:

1) the inclusion in an advanced notice of proposed rulemaking, if issued, of a statement that the proposed rule may have a significant economic effect on a substantial number of small entities;

2) the publication of general notice of proposed rulemaking in publications likely to be obtained by small entities;

3) the direct notification of interested small entities;

4) the conduct of open conferences or public hearings concerning the rule for small entities; and

5) the adoption or modification of agency procedural rules to reduce the cost or complexity of participation in the rulemaking by small entities.

§ 610. Periodic review of rules

a) Within one hundred and eighty days after the effective date of this chapter, each agency shall publish in the Federal Register a plan for the periodic review of the rules issued by the agency which have or will have a significant economic impact upon a substantial number of small entities. Such plan may be amended by the agency at any time by publishing the revision in the Federal Register. The purpose of the review shall be to determine whether such rules should be continued without change, or should be amended or rescinded, consistent with the stated objectives of applicable statutes, to minimize any significant economic impact of the rules upon a substantial number of such small entities. The plan shall provide for the review of all such agency rules existing on the effective date of this chapter within ten years of that date and for the review of such rules adopted after the effective date of this chapter within ten years of the publication of such rules as the final rule. If the head of the agency determines that completion of the review of existing rules is not feasible by the established date, he shall so certify in a statement published in the Federal Register and may extend the completion date by one year at a time for a total of not more than five years.

b) In reviewing rules to minimize any significant economic impact of the rule on a substantial number of small entities in a manner consistent with the stated objectives of applicable statutes, the agency shall consider the following factors –

1) the continued need for the rule;
2) the nature of complaints or comments received concerning the rule from the public;
3) the complexity of the rule;
4) the extent to which the rule overlaps, duplicates or conflicts with other Federal rules, and, to the extent feasible, with State and local governmental rules; and
5) the length of time since the rule has been evaluated or the degree to which technology, economic conditions, or other factors have changed in the area affected by the rule.

Each year, each agency shall publish in the Federal Register a list of the rules which have a significant economic impact on a substantial number of small entities, which are to be reviewed pursuant to this section during the succeeding twelve months. The list shall include a brief description of each rule and the need for and legal basis of such rule and shall invite public comment upon the rule.

§ 611. Judicial review

a) Except as otherwise provided in subsection (b), any determination by an agency concerning the applicability of any of the provisions of this chapter to any action of the agency shall not be subject to judicial review.

b) Any regulatory flexibility analysis prepared under sections 603 and 604 of this title and the compliance or noncompliance of the agency with the provisions of this chapter shall not be subject to judicial review. When an action for judicial review of a rule is instituted, any regulatory flexibility analysis for such rule shall constitute part of the whole record of agency action in connection with the review.

c) Nothing in this section bars judicial review of any other impact statement or similar analysis required by any other law if judicial review of such statement or analysis is otherwise provided by law.

§ 612. Reports and intervention rights

a) The Chief Counsel for Advocacy of the Small Business Administration shall monitor agency compliance with this chapter and shall report at least annually thereon to the President and to the Committees on the Judiciary of the Senate and House of Representatives, the Select Committee on Small Business of the Senate, and the Committee on Small Business of the House of Representatives.

b) The Chief Counsel for Advocacy of the Small Business Administration is authorized to appear as amicus curiae in any action brought in a court of the United States to review a rule. In any such action, the Chief Counsel is authorized to present his views with respect to the effect of the rule on small entities.

c) A court of the United States shall grant the application of the Chief Counsel for Advocacy of the Small Business Administration to appear in any such action for the purposes described in subsection (b).".

EFFECTIVE DATE

SEC. 4. The provisions of this Act shall take effect January 1, 1981, except that the requirements of sections 603 and 604 of title 5, United States Code (as added by section 3 of this Act) shall apply only to rules for which a notice of proposed rulemaking is issued on or after January 1, 1981.

Approved September 19, 1980.

XI. PRESIDENTIAL ORDER FOR FEDERAL REGULATION

Executive Order 12291 of February 17, 1981
Federal Register, Vol. 46, No. 33

By the authority vested in me as President by the Constitution and laws of the United States of America, and in order to reduce the burdens of existing and future regulations, increase agency accountability for regulatory actions, provide for presidential oversight of the regulatory process, minimize duplication and conflict of regulations, and insure well-reasoned regulations, it is hereby ordered as follows:

Section 1. *Definitions.* For the purposes of this Order:

a) "Regulation" or "rule" means an agency statement of general applicability and future effect designed to implement, interpret, or prescribe law or policy or describing the procedure or practice requirements of an agency, hut does not include:
   1. Administrative actions governed by the provisions of Sections 556 and 557 of Title 5 of the United States Code;
   2. Regulations issued with respect to a military or foreign affairs function of the United States; or
   3. Regulations related to agency organization, management, or personnel.

b) "Major rule" means any regulation that is likely to result in:

   1. An annual effect on the economy of $100 million or more;
   2. A major increase in costs or prices for consumers, individual industries, Federal, State, or local government agencies, or geographic regions; or
   3. Significant adverse effects on competition, employment, investment, productivity, innovation, or on the ability of United States-based enterprises to compete with foreign-based enterprises in domestic or export markets.

c) "Director" means the Director of the Office of Management and Budget.

d) "Agency" means any authority of the United States that is an "agency" under 44 U.S.C. 3502q), excluding those agencies specified in 44 U.S.C. 3502(10).

e) "Task Force means the Presidential Task Force on Regulatory Relief.

Sec. 2. *General Requirements.* In promulgating new regulations, reviewing existing regulations, and developing legislative proposals concerning regulation, all agencies, to the extent permitted by law, shall adhere to the following requirements:

a) Administrative decisions shall be based on adequate information concerning *the* need for and consequences of proposed government action;

b) Regulatory action shall not be undertaken unless the potential benefits to society for the regulation outweigh the potential costs to society;

c) Regulatory objectives shall be chosen to maximize the net benefits to society; (d) Among alternative approaches to any given regulatory objective, the alternative involving the least net cost to society shall be chosen; and

d) Agencies shall set regulatory priorities with the aim of maximizing the aggregate net benefits to society, taking into account the condition of the particular industries affected by regulations, the condition of the national economy, and other regulatory actions contemplated for the future.

Sec. 3. Regulatory Impact Analysis and Review

a) In order to implement Section 2 of this Order, each agency shall, in connection with every major rule, prepare, and to the extent permitted by law consider, a Regulatory Impact Analysis. Such Analyses may be combined with any Regulatory Flexibility Analyses performed under 5 U.S.C. 603 and 604.

b) Each Agency shall initially determine whether a rule it intends to propose or to issue is a major rule, provided that, the Director, subject to the directions of the Task Force, shall have authority, in accordance with Sections 1(b) and 2 of the Order, to prescribe criteria for making such determinations, to order a rule to be treated as a major rule, and to require any set of related rules to be considered together as a major rule.

c) Except as provided in Section 8 of this Order, agencies shall prepare Regulatory Impact Analyses of major rules and transmit them, along with all notices of proposed rulemaking and all final rules, to the Director as follows:

1) If no notice of proposed rulemaking is to be published for a proposed major rule that is not an emergency rule, the agency shall prepare only a final Regulatory Impact Analysis, which shall be transmitted, along with the proposed rule, to the Director at least 60 days prior to the publication of the major rule as a final rule;

2) With respect to all other major rules, the agency shall prepare a preliminary Regulatory Impact Analysis, which shall be transmitted, along with a notice of proposed rulemaking, to the Director at least 60 days prior to the publication of a notice of proposed rulemaking, and a final Regulatory Impact Analysis, which shall be transmitted along with the final rule at least 30 days prior to the publication of the major rule as a final rule;

3) For all rules other than major rules, agencies shall submit to the Director, at least 10 days prior to publication, every notice of proposed rulemaking and final rule.

d) To permit each proposed major rule to be analyzed in light of the requirements stated in Section 2 of this Order, each preliminary and final Regulatory Impact Analysis shall contain the following information:

1) A description of the potential benefits of the rule, including any adverse effects that cannot be quantified in monetary terms;

2) A description of the potential costs of the rule, including any adverse effects that cannot be quantified in monetary terms, and the identification of those likely to bear the costs;

3) A determination of the potential net benefits of the rule, including an evaluation of effects that cannot be quantified in monetary terms;

4) A description of alternative approaches that could substantially achieve the same regulatory goal at lower cost, together with an analysis of this potential benefit and costs and a brief explanation of the legal reasons why such alternatives, if proposed, could not be adopted; and

5) Unless covered by the description required under paragraph (4) of this subsection, an explanation of any legal reasons why the rule cannot be based on the requirements set forth in Section 2 of this Order.

e) 1) The Director, subject to the direction of the Task Force, which shall resolve any issues raised under this Order or ensure that they are presented to the President, is authorized to review any preliminary or final Regulatory Impact Analysis, notice of proposed rulemaking, or final rule based on the requirements of this Order.

   2) The Director shall be deemed to have concluded review unless the Director advises an agency to the contrary under subsection (f) of this Section:

      A) Within 60 days of a submission under subsection (c)(1) or a submission of a preliminary Regulatory Impact Analysis or notice of proposed rulemaking under subsection (c)(2);

      B) Within 30 days of the submission of a final Regulatory Impact Analysis and a final rule under subsection (c)(2); and

      C) Within 10 days of the submission of a notice of proposed rulemaking or final rule under subsection (c)(3).

f) 1) Upon the request of the Director, an agency shall consult with the Director concerning the review of a preliminary Regulatory Impact Analysis or notice of proposed rulemaking under this Order, and shall, subject to Section 8(a)(2) of this Order, refrain from publishing its preliminary Regulatory Impact Analysis or notice of proposed rulemaking until such review is concluded.

   2) Upon receiving notice that the Director intends to submit views with respect to any final Regulatory Impact Analysis or final rule, the agency shall, subject to Section 8(a)(2) of this Order, refrain from publishing its final Regulatory Impact Analysis or final rule until the agency has responded to the Director's views, and incorporated those views and the agency's response in the rulemaking file.

   3) Nothing in this subsection shall be construed as displacing the agencies' responsibilities delegated by law.

g) For every rule for which an agency publishes a notice of proposed rulemaking, the agency shall include in its notice:

   1) A brief statement setting forth the agency's initial determination whether the proposed rule is a major rule,

together with the reasons underlying that determination; and
2) For each proposed major rule, a brief summary of the agency's preliminary Regulatory Impact Analysis.

h) Agencies shall make their preliminary and final Regulatory Impact Analyses available to the public.
i) Agencies shall initiate reviews of currently effective rules in accordance with the purposes of this Order, and perform Regulatory Impact Analyses of currently effective major rules. The Director, subject to the direction of the Task Force, may designate currently effective rules for review in accordance with this Order, and establish schedules for reviews and Analyses under this Order.

Sec. 4. *Regulatory Review.* Before approving any final major rule, each agency shall:
a) Make a determination that the regulation is clearly within the authority delegated by law and consistent with congressional intent, and include in the Federal Register at the time of promulgation a memorandum of law supporting that determination.
b) Make a determination that the factual conclusions upon which the rule is based have substantial support in the agency record, viewed as a whole, with full attention to public comments in general and the comments of persons directly affected by the rule in particular.

Sec. 5. *Regulatory Agendas.*

a) Each agency shall publish, in October and April of each year, an agenda of proposed regulations that the agency has issued or expects to issue, and currently effective rules that are under agency review pursuant to this Order. These agendas may be incorporated with the agendas published under 5 U.S.C. 602, and must contain at the minimum:

1) A summary of the nature of each major rule being considered, the objectives and legal basis for the issuance of the rule, and an approximate schedule for completing action on any major rule for which the agency has issued a notice of proposed rulemaking;
2) The name and telephone number of a knowledgeable agency official for each item on the agenda; and
3) A list of existing regulations to be reviewed under the terms

of this Order, and a brief discussion of each such regulation.

b) The Director, subject to the direction of the Task Force, may, to the extent permitted by law:

1) Require agencies to provide additional information in an agenda; and

2) Require publication of the agenda in any form.

Sec. 6. *The Task Force and Office of Management and Budget.*

a) To the extent permitted by law, the Director shall have authority, subject to the direction of the Task Force, to:

1) Designate any proposed or existing rule as a major rule in accordance with Section 1(b) of this Order;

2) Prepare and promulgate uniform standards for the identification of major rules and the development of Regulatory Impact Analyses;

3) Require an agency to obtain and evaluate, in connection with a regulation, any additional relevant data from any appropriate source;

4) Waive the requirements of Sections 3, 4, or 7 of this Order with respect to any proposed or existing major rule;

5) Identify duplicative; overlapping and conflicting rules, existing or proposed, and existing or proposed rules that are inconsistent with the policies underlying statutes governing agencies other than the issuing agency or with the purposes of this Order, and, in each such case, require appropriate interagency consultation to minimize or eliminate such duplication, overlap, or conflict;

6) Develop procedures for estimating the annual benefits and costs of agency regulations, on both an aggregate and economic or industrial sector basis, for purposes of compiling a regulatory budget;

7) In consultation with interested agencies, prepare for consideration by the President recommendations for changes in the agencies' statutes; and

8) Monitor agency compliance with the requirements of this Order and advise the President with respect to such compliance.

b) The Director, subject to the direction of the Task Force, is authorized to establish procedures for the performance of all functions vested in the Director by this Order. The Director shall take appropriate steps to coordinate the implementation of the analysis, transmittal, review, and clearance provisions of this Order with the authorities and requirements provided for or imposed upon the Director and agencies under the Regulatory Flexibility Act, 5 U.S.C. 601 et seq., and the Paperwork Reduction Plan Act of 1980, 44 U.S.C. 3501 et seq.

Sec. 7. *Pending Regulations.*

a) To the extent necessary to permit reconsideration in accordance with this Order, agencies shall, except as provided in Section 8 of this Order, suspend or postpone the effective dates of all major rules that they have promulgated in final form as of the date of this Order, but that have not yet become effective, excluding:

1) Major rules that cannot legally be postponed or suspended;
2) Major rules that, for good cause, ought to become effective as final rules without reconsideration. Agencies shall prepare, in accordance with Section 3 of this Order, a final Regulatory Impact Analysis for each major rule that they suspend or postpone.

b) Agencies shall report to the Director no later than 15 days prior to the effective date of any rule that the agency has promulgated in final form as of the date of this Order, and that has not yet become effective, and that will not be reconsidered under subsection (a) of this Section:

1) That the rule is excepted from reconsideration under subsection (a), including a brief statement of the legal or other reasons for that determination; or
2) That the rule is not a major rule.

c) The Director, subject to the direction of the Task Force, is authorized, to the extent permitted by law, to:

1) Require reconsideration, in accordance with this Order, of any major rule that an agency has issued in final form as of the date of this Order and that has not become effective; and
2) Designate a rule that an agency has issued in final form as of the date of this Order and that has not yet become effective as a major rule in accordance with Section 1(b) of this Order.

d) Agencies may, in accordance with the Administrative Procedure Act and other applicable statutes, permit major rules that they have issued in final form as of the date of this Order, and that have not yet become effective, to take effect as interim rules while they are being reconsidered in accordance with this Order, *provided that,* agencies shall report to the Director, no later than 15 days before any such rule is proposed to take effect as an interim rule, that the rule should appropriately take effect as an interim rule while the rule is under reconsideration.

e) Except as provided in Section 8 of this Order, agencies shall, to the extent permitted by law, refrain from promulgating as a final rule any proposed major rule that has been published or issued as of the date of this Order until a final Regulatory Impact Analysis, in accordance with Section 3 of this Order, has been prepared for the proposed major rule.

f) Agencies shall report to the Director, no later than 30 days prior to promulgating as a final rule any proposed rule that the agency has published or issued as of the date of this Order and that has not been considered under the terms of this Order:

1) That the rule cannot legally be considered in accordance with this Order, together with a brief explanation of the legal reasons barring such consideration; or

2) That the rule is not a major rule, in which case the agency shall submit to the Director a copy of the proposed rule.

g) The Director, subject to the direction of the Task Force, is authorized, to the extent permitted by law, to:

1) Require consideration, in accordance with this Order, of any proposed major rule that the agency has published or issued as of the date of this Order; and (2) Designate a proposed rule that an agency has published or issued as of the date of this Order, as a major rule in accordance with Section 1(b) of this Order.

h) The Director shall be deemed to have determined that an agency's report to the Director under subsections (b), (d), or (f) of this Section is consistent with the purposes of this Order, unless the Director advises *the* agency to the contrary:

1) Within 15 days of its report, in the case of any report under subsections (b) or (d); or

2) Within 30 days of its report, in the case of any report under subsection (f).

i) This Section does not supersede the President's Memorandum of January 29, 1981, entitled "Postponement of Pending Regulations", which shall remain in effect until March 30, 1981.

j)   In complying with this Section, agencies shall comply with all applicable provisions of the Administrative Procedure Act, and with any other procedural requirements made applicable to the agencies by other statutes.

Sec. 8. **Exemptions.**

a)   The procedures prescribed by this Order shall not apply to:

1)   Any regulation that responds to an emergency situation, provided *that,* any such regulation shall be reported to the Director as soon as is practicable, the agency shall publish in the Federal Register a statement of the reasons why it is impracticable for the agency to follow the procedures of this Order with respect to such a rule, and the agency shall prepare and transmit as soon as is practicable a Regulatory Impact Analysis of any such major rule; and

2)   Any regulation for which consideration or reconsideration under the terms of this Order would conflict with deadlines imposed by statute or by judicial order, *provided that,* any such regulation shall be reported to the Director together with a brief explanation of the conflict, the agency shall publish in the Federal Register a statement of the reasons why it is impracticable for the agency to follow the procedures of this Order with respect to such a rule, and the agency, in consultation with the Director, shall adhere to the requirements of this Order to the extent permitted by statutory or judicial deadlines,

b)   The Director, subject to the direction of the Task Force, may, in accordance with the purposes of this Order, exempt any class or category of regulations from any or all requirements of this Order.

Sec. 9 **Judicial Review.** This Order is intended only to improve the internal management of the Federal government, and is not intended to create any right or benefit, substantive or procedural, enforceable at law by a party against the United States, its agencies, its officers or any person. The determinations made by agencies under Section 4 of this Order, and any Regulatory Impact Analyses for any rule, shall be made part of the whole record of agency action in connection with the rule.

SEC. 10. *REVOCATIONS.* EXECUTIVE ORDERS NO. 12044, AS AMENDED, AND NO. 12174 ARE REVOKED. THE WHITE HOUSE, *February 17, 1981.*

TABLE OF CASES

TABLE OF STATUTES

INDEX

L/R

We welcome your comments on this publication. Please write us at Staff@LawReviewPublishing.com.

If you are an excellent student, please inquire about our student editor positions. We can be reached at (800) 371-1271.